Motivational Interviewing Workbook:

Treating Sexual Offending Across the Spectrum of Acceptance

Mark S. Carich, PhD

Jessie K. Huebner, PhD

March 2023

Motivational Interviewing Workbook: Treating Across the Spectrum of Acceptance

Copyright © 2023 Carich & Huebner
All rights reserved.
ISBN-13: 9798387590634

Table of Contents

Preface 1

Chapter 1: Introduction 5

Chapter 2: What Happened? Clarifying the Current Situation & Extent of The Issues 15

Chapter 3: Current Treatment- Good Lives Model 23

Chapter 4: Change 35

Chapter 5: Rethinking Your Thinking 43

Chapter 6: Interpersonal Relationship Skills & Empathy 55

Chapter 7: Regulation Skills & Mood Management 61

Chapter 8: Behavioral Impact & Empathy 71

Chapter 9: Arousal Control & Sexual Regulation Skills 79

Chapter 10: Addressing Trauma- Core Issues 85

Chapter 11: Pattern Identification: Selecting Pathways 95

Chapter 12: Meta-Change Maintenance: Preserving Change and Staying on Track 103

Chapter 13: Concluding Thoughts 125

References 127

Motivational Interviewing Workbook: Treating Across the Spectrum of Acceptance

Preface

Treatment is required in most courts for individuals who sexually offend. Some clients will readily admit to the offense, while others will not. People that do not admit, for whatever reason, can still receive effective treatment. This module is the nuts and bolts of treatment for clients who will not admit. We realize that denial is not a risk factor. This module will help the client make some changes, at minimum, to the effect of never getting into this predicament again.

This module is partly based on Ward's (2002) Good Lives Model (GLM). The GLM model suggests that individuals have two life plans: (a) fragmented chaotic life plan, in which, needs are inappropriately met and there is an attempt to cope with life by drug use, criminal behavior, aggression, sexual offending and (b) a coherent responsible life plan, in which, one meets needs appropriately, making reasonable decisions. Some people go back and forth between their two life plans.

This module is based on several assumptions:

- Treatment involves a holistic view of the person/client, where deviant behavior is only one aspect of self. We realize, quite often, the impact of offending is devastating.
- The construct of denial is multi-leveled and dimensional: commonly defined as not admitting to something with another facet of not taking responsibility.
- Denial, in general, is not correlated with risk according to the classic Hanson (2014) meta-analysis on risk and recidivism.
- There are typical reasons or purposes of denial (e.g., shame, avoiding consequences, not wanting to deal with the behavior).
- Denial and/or avoiding accountability of offenses, does not have to impede therapy
- Treatment can be successfully done with people in denial.

Therapist Notes on "Denial"

Treatment Issues

- Historically, deniers were excluded from and/or terminated from treatment.
- Prior treatment culture consisted of shame based intensive confrontation
- We now realize that records and versions of the events may vary
- Responsivity is the key: being responsive to the client's needs, situation, experiences...
- Denial/responsibility may be a mitigating factor for successful treatment

- Not recommended to kick out a client due to denial (Marshall et al., 2006; Marshall et al., 2011)
- For incest/family abuse, client needs to take responsibility for offenses to help family heal at the highest level.

Research Issues

- Research is often muddled and conflicting
- Hanson & Bussiere (1998) and Hanson & Morton-Bourgon (2005) found that denial is not associated with risk or recidivism
- Barbaree, Langton et. al. (2008) found that if denial is viewed on a continuum, then it is associated with risk versus a binary view which is not associated with risk
- Lund (2000) found several problems with the Hanson research (e.g., only studies had denial in them, definitions varied)
- Yates (2009) summarized the research indicating denial maybe a natural healthy response and a protective factor.
- Yates (2009) summary includes:
  - Incest deniers seem to be at higher risk than admitters, but overall re-offend at lower rates (Nunes et. al., 2007)
  - With unrelated victims, deniers re-offend at lower risks than admitters
  - Low risk offenders were more likely to re-offend compared to admitters
  - High risk deniers re-offend at lower rates compared to admitters
- Schema-based theory differentiates core schemas (cognitive structures, processes) representing underlying views and attitudes
  - Cognitive distortions are the products of schemas
- Schneider and Wright (2004) found denial was correlated with treatment advancement
- Marshall, Marshall, et al. (2011) conducted a categorical denier program versus admitter program, and found that the denier program had had lower recidivism rates than admitter program (both were very low anyway)
- In terms of other Dynamic Risk Factors (DRFs) not correlated with risk, Marshall and colleagues found deficits in various areas

Approaches

- Use as-if/what-if situation happened and you did it
- Use the hypothetical "I did it" throughout treatment
- Explore the situation looking multiple factors
- Look at how you got into the situation
- Run through treatment to prevent you from ever getting accused again
- Emphasis on current and future responsibility

Conclusions

- Yates (2009) suggests that denial is a healthy response
- The key is focusing on core schemas and/or implicit theories
- Denial manifests itself in multiple ways (e.g., cognitive distortions, defenses)
- The research is inconsistent
- How denial is viewed and handled is often based upon the professional
- Denial serves different purposes
- Some constructs are multi-level and dimensional
- Need better standard definitions of specific DRFs

The goals of this module include:

- Decrease the potential for sexual aggression.
- To help clients avoid getting into offending potential situations.
- To help clients help enhance living their pro-social life plan.
- To help clients engage in some self reflection.

Chapter 1
Introduction

Life is quite complex, involving any number of problems and issues, along with complex decisions. Likewise, crossing the line sexually involves complex decisions with simpler interventions.

Given that you are doing this workbook, something likely happened with a sexual tone. There are several possible things. Either the legal system or court system is involved (including the supervising officer, states attorney, judge, etc.) wanting you to attend treatment, based upon allegations, charges, and/or convictions. Typically, there are several versions of what happened because people are involved and typically have different experiences.

This workbook will help you clarify what happened and your decision-making processes. It has been designed to help you look your decisions to cross sexual lines (boundaries) and help you make better decisions in the future. This workbook can also be a guide to improve your emotional regulation skills, mood management skills, and identify plans to prevent engaging in problematic sexual actions or behaviors going forward. This workbook is meant to act as a guide and does not necessarily need to be completed in the order presented.

What Is This Workbook about?

This workbook is to be used with a therapist or mental health worker. Some areas or topics may be a bit touchy and could be emotionally charged. You may need help with them. More specifically, this workbook will help you:

- Figure out who you are and what you are about
- How you meet your needs
- Your pathways in life
- How to develop and maintain relationships
- How to re-think your thinking that might not work as well
- How to manage your emotions
- How to cope with life and meet your needs appropriately
- How to maintain change

What Is Sexual Aggression?

Sexual aggression can mean many things. There are different definitions and sometimes can be confusing, especially when relationships are involved.

Task 1.1 What does sexual aggression mean to you?

_____
_____
_____
_____
_____
_____
_____

Sexual aggression is simply violating someone else sexually. This means hurting someone else sexually. In other words, it means the sexual behavior is unwarranted (not wanted) or the person couldn't or didn't consent to it. There are several key elements involved to help define it. These include:

- Person doesn't want to have sex (or do sexual acts)
- Person isn't of age
- Person is disabled and can't make decisions
- Person can't make decisions
- Person isn't aware

There is an impact as you might already have experienced.

Task 1.2 What do you think the impact of sexual aggression is? How could the outcome affect others?

_____
_____
_____
_____
_____
_____
_____

Sexual aggression can be looked at on a range or continuum of behaviors ranging from noncontact (means literally no hands-on) to hands-on (or contact) offenses. This idea is displayed in Figure#1.

Continuum of Offending

Range of Offenses

Non-contact--------------------------------Contact

- **Non-contact Offenses** (hands off) (covert)
  - **Non-physical contact**
- **Contact offenses** (hands on) (overt)
  - **Involves Physical Contact**

Figure 1. Range of Offending Behavior

Table 1. Types of Contact Vs. Non-Contact Offenses

Non-contact Offenses	Contact Offenses
Obscene phone calling	Physical sexual harassment
Stalking	Fondling (Frottage)
Peeping	Child Molestation (sex with children)
Flashing (exhibitionism)	Date rape
Verbal sexual harassment	Sadistic rape
Unwarranted computer sex	Relationship/spousal rape
Photography (unwanted)	Bestiality
Pornography	Sexual attempt murder
Mail/computer sex	Sexual murder
Sexting-Texting/sending images	Serial sexual murder
That aren't warranted/unwanted	Necrophilia (sex with the dead)

What Goes into Sexual Aggression or an Offense?

There are a number of potential elements that go into offending. These are commonly referred to as risk factors. You will hear a lot about risk factors. Risk factors are simply: any internal event (inside of you) or external (in your environment) that brings someone closer to committing an offense. These can be historical (called static because they don't change) and dynamic (factors that change, such as thinking, sexual behavior, relationships, coping skills,...). You can't change history. But by making changes in the dynamic factors you or anyone can reduce their risk. Below is a laundry list of risk factors (Carich, Huebner, & May, 2020; Carich, Huebner, & Loy, 2020; Carich, May, & Huebner, 2020a; Hanson & Yates, 2013; Mann et al., 2010):

Historical Factors:

- Prior history of criminally charged sex offenses
- Number of victims
- Length of time offending
- Stranger victims
- Male child victim only
- Male child victim
- History of being sexually abused
- Diverse documented criminal history
- Used a weapon during sex offense
- Disciplinary problems in school
- History of sexualized violence in charges
- Planned offense

6 Factorial Domains

Below is Carich, Huebner, & Loy (2020) re-categorization of meaningful dynamic risk factors originally presented by Mann et al. (2010)

- Deviant Sexual Interest, Sexual Related Issues and Arousal Management
- Cognitive Factors
    - Externalized Coping**
    - Basic Cognitive Tactics
    - Implicit Theories
- Interpersonal Relationship and Social Factors

- Intellectual or Cognitive Level of Empathy for Victims
- General Regulation Skills (relates to self-management)
- Lifestyle Behaviors – Antisociality and Other Related

Deviant Sexual Interest, Sexual Related Issues and Arousal Management
- Sexual pre-occupation*
- Any deviant sexual interest*
- Sexual preference for children*
- Sadism/ coercive sex* (Sexualized violence arousal)
- Sexualized coping**
- Poor arousal control*** (sexual regulation skills)
- Sexual entitlement***

Cognitive Factors (& Responsibility)
- Responsibility for offenses
- Cognitive distortions
- Overall attitude
- Externalized Coping**:
    - Justifying/Minimization – excuses and making less
    - Entitlement – Unrealistic expectations placed on self/others
    - Extreme thinking – either/or rigid, concrete, castastrophizing/awfulizing
    - Assuming/mind reading – reading into how others are thinking without knowing
    - Illusion of control – Illusion one has to control to be okay
    - Victim stance – based on fairness fallacy (life ain't fair), playing victim role
    - Narcissistic– Everything has to center around me ("I'm the best" or superior to everyone)
- Basic Cognitive Tactics:
    - Denial – Non-Admission, not taking responsibility
    - Power games/Controlling others- dominating based on Illusion one has to control to be okay
    - Lying – Making up untruths and acting as if they are true
    - Playing confused
    - Scorekeeping – Keeping track of errors others make and/or wrongdoings made by others towards you
    - Using Anger
    - Blaming – Placing your/others responsibility onto others
    - Closed channel – Being non-receptive

– Ally seeking – Getting others on one's side to validate your point
- Offense supportive attitudes* also referred to as Implicit Theories (beliefs involving offenses or blueprint beliefs):
    – Women are deceptive
    – Disrespect towards some women
    – Women/kids are primarily sex objects
    – Illusion of control (one has to control others & context)
    – Sees self as a victim
    – Grievance & hostility towards others
    – Views self as inadequate (poor self-esteem)
    – Sex drive is uncontrollable
    – Sexual entitlement
    – Nature of harm (non-overt violence means NO harm, minimizes impact)
    – Dangerous world view (lack of trust, paranoia, adults=dangerous, need to control others)

Interpersonal Relationship and Social Factors
- Emotional Congruence/ identifies with children**
- Lack of emotional intimate relationships with adults* (isolated)
- Social skills***
- Conflicts within intimate relationships*
- Negative social influences* (vs. positive)
- Loneliness***
- Empathy related (understanding of other's perspective)***

Intellectual or Cognitive Level of Empathy for Victims
- Emotional levels of empathy for victims
- Emotional Factors
- Grievance/Hostility*
- Hostility towards women**
- Emotional regulation skills*
    – Emotional instability
    – Harbors negative emotional states

General Regulation Skills (relates to Self-Management)

- Poor problem solving skills*
- Dysfunctional coping- irrational**
- Dysfunctional coping- emotion dominated**

- Understands patterns and has coping responses in place
- Compliance with rules and treatment*
    - Non-compliance with basic rules*
    - Challenges rules*
    - Refuses groups/program activities

Lifestyle Behaviors – Antisociality & Other Related

- Lifestyle Impulsivity*
- Recklessness*
- Callousness/Lack of concern for others** (empathy related)
- Self Concept & Related Core Issues*** (including, self-esteem isn't, however this often makes the difference in treatment)
- Male Machiavellianism** (Controlling, dominating, doing whatever to get one's way)
- Employment instability*
- Childhood behavioral problems and early delinquency*

* Indicates Research Supported
**Indicates Promising Research Supported Factors
***Indicates large bodies of research indicates deficits, however, not directly linked to sexual recidivism.

Through treatment, you will address the risk factors that apply to you, thus making changes in your life. In treatment, we look at your whole life. You, and anyone else in treatment for sexual offending, are not defined as a "SEX OFFENDER". Committing a sexual transgression or offending behavior is only one aspect of a person. This treatment workbook takes this into consideration.

Task 1.3 Circle the factors from above that you think might apply to you. If you decide not to admit, go ahead a circle factors that either pertain or would pertain had you admitted that you done it.

Task 1.4 Write about how they apply and process with a therapist

_____
_____
_____
_____

A Brief Overview of What Treatment Is?

   Treatment is a therapy or therapeutic process to help you make changes. You are the only one that can make changes. The therapist can't do it for you. There is no magic to it. We have provided a number of tasks to help you make changes in your life, to live a better life without sexual aggression.

Task 1.5 Do you think you need to make changes in your life? Why?

Task 1.6 What types of changes do you think you need to make?

_____
_____
_____
_____
_____
_____
_____

Task 1.7 What are the pros/benefits of making changes?

_____
_____
_____
_____
_____
_____
_____
_____
_____
_____
_____

The model is described in Chapter 3. It involves a Cognitive-Behavioral Therapy (CBT) Approach combined with Positive Psychology through the Good Lives Model. Treatment is approached from more of a positive view, recognizing your human potential and strengths. The approach is more of a CBT+ model, focusing on thoughts, feelings, behaviors, relationships, and your potential. Typically, groups are used to help provide valuable feedback and support.

The overall goals include:

- Enhancing your pro-social life plan
    - Learning about yourself
    - Taking responsibility for self currently and in your future
    - Meeting your needs appropriately
    - Learning effective coping skills
    - Learning to enhance your relationships and skills
    - Learning to manage your emotions better
    - Identifying your functional and dysfunctional pathways
    - Learning how to preserve the changes you have made
- No more victims
- Harm reduction

Chapter 2
What Happened? Clarifying the Current Situation & Extent of The Issues

As mentioned earlier, given that you are doing this workbook, something happened with a sexual tone. There are several possible things. Either the legal system or court system is involved (including the supervising officer, states attorney, judge, etc.) wanting you to attend treatment, based upon allegations, charges, and/or convictions. Typically, there are several versions of what happened because people are involved and typically have different experiences.

Clarifying What Happened

We don't know what happened. Only you and the persons involved actually know. You will have to ask yourself if you are willing to be honest or not with yourself and others. Below are several assignments to help you with that. Be as honest as you can be.

In general, a sexual offense is any sexually oriented behavior that violates another's boundaries, thus hurting another person. It is a sexual transgression, or violation of another's rights through sexual means. Based upon this definition, answer the following questions.

Task 2.1 What happened that brought you here?

_____
_____
_____
_____
_____
_____
_____
_____
_____
_____
_____
_____
_____
_____

Task 2.2 What did the "victim" or system say happened?

Task 2.3 What do you say happened?

Task 2.4 What did the authorities say happened?

Task 2.5 If there is a difference, why?

The Issue of Denial or Responsibility

It is quite normal to deny or avoid admitting to stuff that you don't want to admit to because perhaps you are embarrassed, having difficulties facing what happened or the pain involved, or you simply want to avoid the hurt of what happened. Perhaps you want to get out of what happened or maybe nothing happened. Ultimately, it is going to be up to you to be honest about your experiences. No one can force you to do anything. Several exercises are designed to help you sort this out. At any rate, we do not want you to make stuff up. Rather you admit to what happened or not, this workbook will help you. Taking current and future responsibility for life is key.

Task 2.6 What would happen if you did admit to whatever happened?

Task 2.7 What would happen if you didn't admit to it?

Task 2.8 What would be some reasons for not admitting to what happened and your role/part?

Task 2.9 What are the pros/benefits of admitting to your part?

Task 2.10 What would be the cons if you don't admit your part?

_____
_____
_____
_____

In the event that you actually didn't do it or for whatever reason are reluctant to admit to what happened, answer the questions or tasks in this workbook "as If" you did it. This is called using a hypothetical "as if" approach. It takes a lot of courage to face up to what one has done!

Shame

Task 2.11 Sometimes people will not admit to stuff they did because of intense shame. Is that your situation? ____yes ___no ____maybe

Task 2.12 If so, describe your feelings about the situation.

_____
_____
_____
_____
_____
_____
_____

Task 2.13 If so, how can you resolve those feelings.

1. _____
2. _____
3. _____
4. _____
5. _____
6. _____
7. _____
8. _____

Toxic Shame

In this section, we are looking at how you are feeling up to this point. Remorse is different than toxic shame. Feeling guilty after violating someone is still considered normal. However, when you get to the point of feeling bad about yourself and that you are no good—that actually crosses the line into toxic shame. Toxic shame is the feeling of worthlessness. Your behavior is not the end of the world; however, there are usually impacts. Many people find it a relief to talk about what happened to a trusted person. It lifts the burden. The following tasks will help you sort through toxic shame—if you are experiencing it.

Task 2.14 What are you experiencing?

_____
_____
_____
_____
_____
_____
_____

Task 2.15 If you are experiencing toxic shame, how can you deal with it?

_____
_____
_____
_____
_____
_____
_____
_____

Perhaps you would feel better by giving back, also called restitution, and making changes in your life so you don't hurt others in the future. Talk to your therapist.

Task 2.16 How could you give back? How could you make amends?

_____
_____
_____
_____
_____

_____
_____
_____
_____

Task 2.17 How does that feel? (Discuss with a therapist)

_____
_____
_____
_____
_____
_____
_____
_____
_____

Chapter 3
Current Treatment- Good Lives Model

Introduction

It is important to understand the theory and/or theoretical assumptions of self, change, and treatment. In this chapter, we outline our thinking about change and what goes into change. Furthermore, how it applies to you is key. Theory is nothing more than a set of assumptions and viewpoints. This provides a road map.

Human nature can be quite complex. There are multiple views of the human condition. In fact, you yourself actually have one. In your mind, you have constructed how life works and how people work. Your views are usually out of your awareness. We believe in a holistic view of humans, meaning that sexual offending (deviance) is only one part, or aspect, of self. There are other areas of your life. For some, sexual preoccupation is a bigger slice of their life than for others.

Our brief comments on human nature are presented below. The workbook and treatment are based on these views summarize below.

Human Condition

The human condition is complex, with many different views from leading professionals (Adler, 1941; Adler, 1956; Dreikurs, 1967).

As mentioned, most people have some sort of view of why people do what they do and why things happen. It is important that you look at your views and perhaps clarify your thinking. This workbook is based on these assumptions of the human condition or nature can be summarized below:

- People are self-deterministic (make choices at all levels of awareness).
- There are multiple levels of awareness.
- Reality and causality can be viewed in multiple levels and dimensions.
- All aspects of self are connected (holistic view) e.g., mind-body connection
- People continuously evolve and develop (developmental view)
- Behavior is goal-oriented and serves purposes.
- We live in a social context.
- People create their own inner realities.

Holistic View

The essence of our views is that we take a holistic view that the mind and body are connected and can't be separated (Longo, 2002). Each influences the other and can be viewed as one.

With that in mind, people constantly make decisions at both the conscious and unconscious levels of awareness, but we are still held 100% responsible and accountable for our behavior. Likewise, offending is a complex set of decisions involving the mind-body connection. Some people will struggle with deviant urges the rest of their lives, how they are acting out is a choice. You are young and have a chance to shape your arousal to some degree. This varies from person to person.

People develop and evolve over time, collecting a variety of learning experiences. Experiences are encoded through the mind-body memory processes. At the same time, needs are being met and activated. Typically, one gets more out of offending than sexual gratification. There are needs being met during the offense.

There are multiple areas within the self that make up the human experience. They are listed below. These are dimensions or experiential domains of self.

Dimensions of Self

- Multiple experiential domains of self
    - Cognitive – thoughts, ideas, attitudes
    - Affective – emotions, moods, feelings
    - Behavioral – overt (motor) activities
    - Spiritual – connection to higher power/meaning
    - Biological-Physiological – organs, chemistry
    - Socially – attachment, relationships
    - Contextual – background, environmental
    - Sensory Modalities – perceptual modes
- Core: Mind-Body Connection
    - Core Perceptual Belief System (State-Dependent Memory Learning)

When offending, a bio-physiological cascading effect occurs as the other domains are also involved. The holistic view of these experiential domains of self are displayed in Figure 2.

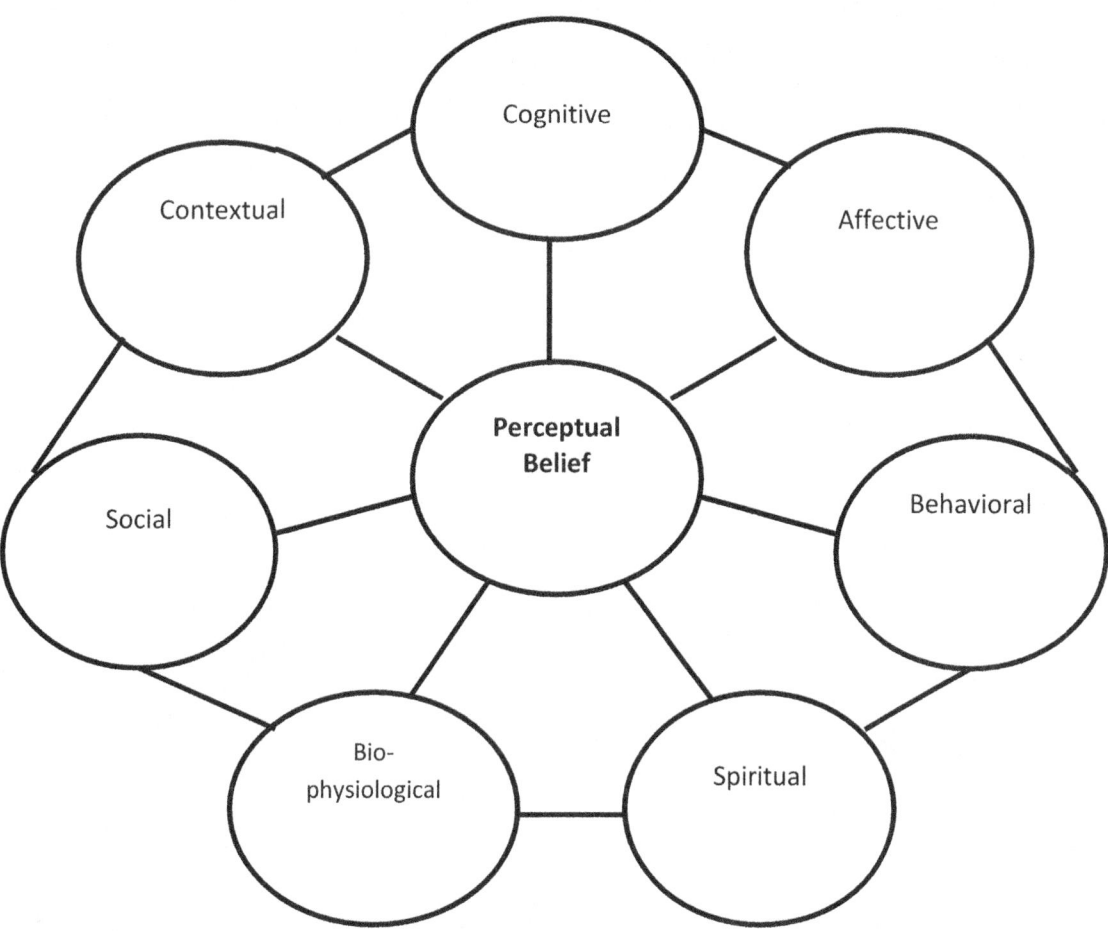

Figure 2: Experiential Domains of Self

As indicated in the figure, each domain is connected to the other and influences the other as well. Some are more present than others. However, the key to all of this is one's perception, which relates to one's belief system. Again, every domain is connected through the mind-body connection.

The other aspect of holistic view and good lives is that you are more than the deviant offending aspect. Although some offenders are consumed with deviancy, and sexually occupied, others are not. It is important for you to figure out the degree of deviancy in your life. There are different parts, or roles, of one's life, including:

- Son
- Father (as you may have a child)
- Intimate relationships

- Extended family members
- Spirituality
- Leisure time
- Work / Employment
- Education- student
- Skill sets
- Interests

There are different roles we play in life and different aspects of our life. We seem to act differently when playing different roles.

Task 3.1 Complete the pie with the different roles you have. For Discussion: How do roles impact our interactions with others? Who are we with others?

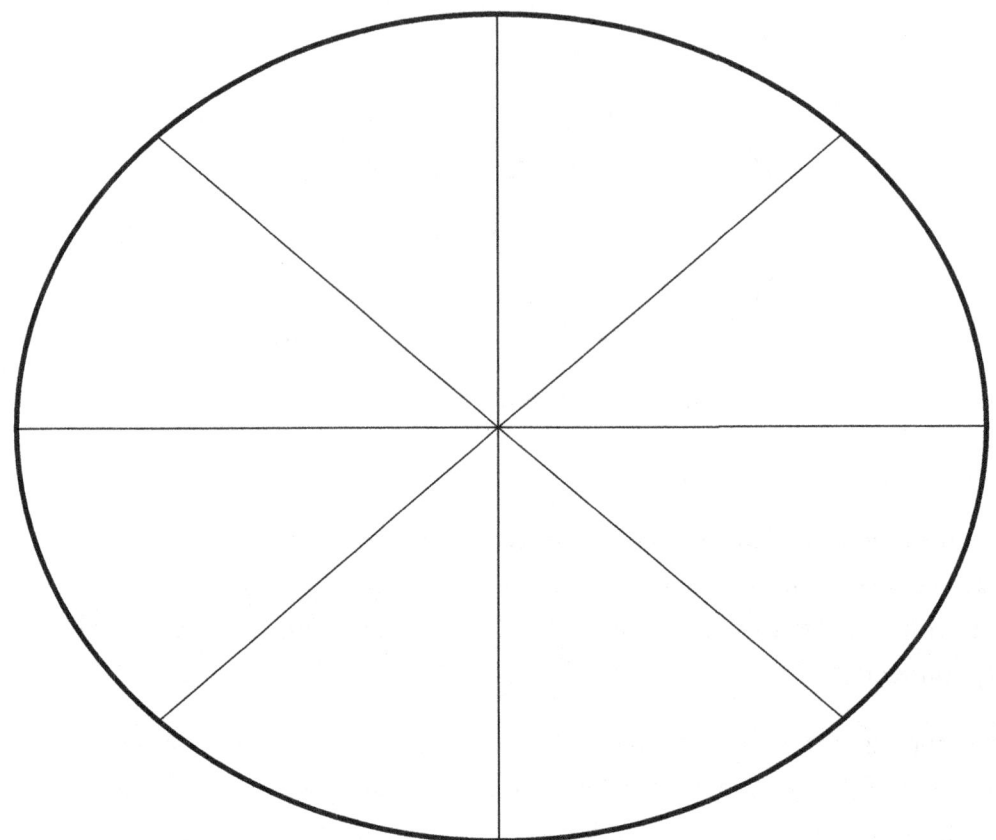

Good Lives Model

The good lives model developed by Tony Ward (2002) and enhanced by Yates, Prescott, and Ward (2010) will help to put all of this together.

The Good Lives Model (GLM) is a positive view of people. In essence, we all have life plans. Some are better than others. Sometimes, life plans take different turns, always based on our decisions (Ward & Stewart, 2003). For a complicated scientific definition, McMurran and Ward (2004) stated: "a core assumption of the model is that all individuals have an implicit or explicit plan that they rely on to structure their lives and to guide everyday actions." In essence, humans are driven by primary goods (needs). Their plans specify core values that guide them in everyday actions. Their plans reflect their personal identity, which dictates their pursuit of goals. This results in an overall sense of purpose or meaning of one's life. If you need a more scientific definition of primary goods, here is one:

> **Primary Goods** – are actions, states of affairs, characteristics, experiences and states of mind that are viewed as intrinsically beneficial to human beings and are sought for their own sake rather than as means to some fundamental ends. These are actions, experiences and activities… that are intrinsically beneficial to people (McMurran & Ward, 2004).

We refer to primary goods as *needs*. Ward and colleagues pose nine different primary goods.

- Life – healthy living, optimal physical functioning, sexual satisfaction
- Knowledge
- Excellence in play/work (i.e., mastery experiences)
- Excellence in agency (i.e., autonomy and self-directedness)
- Inner peace (i.e., freedom from emotional turmoil and stress)
- Friendship and relatedness (intimate, romantic, family relationships and community [connection to others])
- Spirituality (finding meaning and purpose and/or related to a higher power)
- Happiness
- Creativity

Marshall, Marshall, Serran and O'Brien (2011) combined different categories together identifying the following primary goods:

- Health- good diet and exercise

- Mastery- in work and play
- Autonomy- self-directedness
- Relatedness- intimate/sexual relationship, family, friends, kinship, and community
- Inner peace- freedom from turmoil and stress, a sense of purpose and meaning in life
- Knowledge and creativity- satisfaction from knowing and creating things (e.g., job or hobby related knowledge, playing music, writing).

Prescott (2018) offered a summary of "goods" or needs as applied to youth:

- Having Fun
- Being an Achiever
- Being My Own Person
- Being Connected to Other People
- Having a Purpose in Life
- Meeting My Emotional Needs
- Meeting My Sexual Needs
- Being Physically Healthy

Life Plans

There are generally two life plans: fragmented and coherent. People in more fragmented (dysfunctional) life plans tend to be more chaotic; while people living more coherent (functional) plans are meeting needs appropriately. In general, it is about developing and/or maintaining functional life plans. The goal in treatment is to maintain a pro-social life plan, thus remaining trouble-free.

Task 3.2 What does your coherent life plan look like?

_____
_____
_____
_____
_____
_____
_____
_____
_____
_____
_____

_____
_____
_____

Task 3.3 What does your fragmented/chaotic life plan look like?

_____
_____
_____
_____
_____
_____
_____
_____
_____
_____
_____
_____
_____
_____
_____

You need to decide what direction that you want to go in.

Task 3.4 What are your strengths?

1. _____
2. _____
3. _____
4. _____
5. _____
6. _____
7. _____
8. _____

Task 3.5 What are your goals?
_____
_____
_____
_____
_____
_____
_____
_____
_____
_____
_____

Task 3.6 How do you currently meet your needs?
_____
_____
_____
_____
_____
_____
_____
_____
_____

Task 3.7 Complete the grid.

This exercise should highlight changes in your life as well. How are you currently meeting these needs? How did you meet these needs in the past? How do you plan to meet these needs in the future?

Need/Good	Current	Past	Future
1. Healthy living			
2. Knowledge and creativity			

3. Mastery and working in			
4. Autonomy			
5. Inner peace			
6. Spirituality			
7. Relatedness & Interpersonal			

Much of your life plan will rely on how you think, your feeling or mood states, behaviors and relationships… along with how you regulate yourself.

Instrumental or secondary goods provide concrete means to secure primary goods. In sex offender work, criminogenic needs/Dynamic (changeable) Risk Factors (DRFs) are blocks in the acquisition of primary human goods. Therefore, these DRFs are targeted in treatment and can reduce one's risk to re-offending. Sexual offending results from problems in the way goods are secured or sought.

There are four types of problems or difficulties when trying to obtain the nine primary goods. These difficulties result in dysfunctional behavior. The four types of difficulties are:

- **Means** – inappropriate strategies used to secure goods
- **Lack of scope/leaving out goods** – or imbalanced life plan
- **Conflict** – with meeting goods
- **Lack of capability** – no knowledge, skills…

(Yates et al., 2010)

Applied to offending (and any other dysfunctional behavioral patterns), the fragmented life plan has two general routes of offending (Mann et al., 2004:

1. Direct route—directly looking for victims (approach pathway)
2. Indirect route—jumping on opportunities that come to offend or even out of curiosity (avoidant pathway [as you may not be directly looking to offend]).

The direct route involves an approach pathway, or pattern, in which one seeks victims and seems to really enjoy offending. The person in the approach pathway uses skills, manipulation, tricks or even violence to get his fix via victims. The indirect route resembles the avoidant pathway in which one doesn't actually want to offend, yet has poor coping skills and ends up making decisions to offend. Typically, there are two sub-pathways with each strategy (Ward & Hudson, 1998; 2000).

The approach pathway has two sub-pathways:

1. Approach-Explicit, or Active, in which one sets up and continuously seeks victims.
2. Approach-Automatic, or Passive – where one acts out on impulse.

The avoidant pathway includes:

1. Avoidant-Passive, in which one lacks coping skills.
2. Avoidant-Active, in which one's coping skills don't work.

The self-regulation model (SRM) has been integrated with the type of pathways (Yates et al., 2010). What is important for you is to determine what type of overall pathway do you use when in the offending pattern.

It appears that people can jump from coherent to fragmented life plans and back and forth. The point is that a more coherent life plan leads to functional decisions, whereas a fragmented life plan leads to dysfunctional and often destructive decisions.

Conclusion

The bottom line is that the human condition is complex; however, it can be made simple. Everyone continuously makes choices as they evolve through life. Also, behavior serves purposes as people strive to meet needs. Everyone has needs and a life plan. Life plans dictate how we will live our lives and make choices to meet our needs. Life plans are based on beliefs, viewpoints, strategies and needs.

Life plans are either coherent or fragmented. A coherent life plan involves making functional decisions, and, overall, meeting needs appropriately. "Fragmented" means life plans based on dysfunctional ways to meet needs as one meanders through life with choices. Food for thought...ask yourself: how do you currently meet your needs?

Chapter 4
Change

Change is making a difference. Staying the same is not change. Change is recovery. Recovery is developing and maintaining a pro-social life plan and lifestyle. Recovery is creating and maintaining a non-offending lifestyle (Bays & Freeman-Longo, 2000; Carich, 1991; Watzlawick et al., 1974). Change occurs in multiple levels and dimensions (Carich & Dobkowski, 2007; Hanson & Harris, 2001; Prochaska & DiClemente, 1982). Change occurs in the following areas:

- Cognitive or thinking
- Affective or feeling
- Behaviorally or actions
- Socially or interpersonal relationships
- Spiritually and or the meeting and purpose of your life
- Biologically and physiologically – all changes are reflected through your body chemistry as the mind-body are connected.

The point is now, in this stage of your treatment, you think differently than you did before, which in turn creates different feelings. In terms of feeling different, you can now regulate or control your mood better recognize and change or defuse negative mood states quicker. Instead of dysregulated, you are more regulated now as you interact differently developing deeper relationships, without strings attached. Not only that, you are more willing to make these changes. You have a desire to keep these changes. You find meaning in your life and purpose. The last two tie in spiritual aspects of self. Perhaps you found spirituality assigns the purpose and meaning in life; spatiality is also connection to a higher power by realizing that the world is much bigger than us.

This workbook will help you maintain change.

Task 4.1 What areas do you struggle with?

1. _____

2. _____

3. _____

4. _____

5. _____

6. _____

7. _____

8. _____

Task 4.2 List out the PROS & CONS of change.

Pros	Cons

Task 4.3 List out Reasons why you need to change.

1. _____

2. _____

3. _____

4. _____

5. _____

6. _____

7. _____

8. _____

Task 4.4 What do you need to change and why?

What I need to Change	Why

Task 4.5 If there was a miracle, what would be different?

_____
_____
_____
_____
_____
_____
_____
_____
_____

Task 4.6 Since you are here, what do you want to work on?

1. _____
2. _____
3. _____
4. _____
5. _____
6. _____
7. _____
8. _____

Task 4.7 What are some of your barriers to work through?

1. _____
2. _____
3. _____
4. _____
5. _____
6. _____
7. _____
8. _____

Task 4.8 How are you going to overcome them?

Barrier_____

How to overcome it?

- _____

- _____
- _____

Barrier_____

How to overcome it?

- _____
- _____
- _____

Barrier_____

How to overcome it?

- _____
- _____
- _____

Barrier_____

How to overcome it?

- _____
- _____
- _____

Barrier_____

How to overcome it?

- _____
- _____
- _____

Barrier_____

How to overcome it?

- _____
- _____
- _____

Task 4.9 How did you get into your situation?

_____
_____
_____
_____
_____
_____
_____
_____
_____
_____

Task 4.10 How are you going to prevent from ever getting into this type of situation again?

1. _____
2. _____
3. _____
4. _____
5. _____
6. _____

Task 4.11   In summary, what changes do you need to make?

1. _____
2. _____
3. _____

4. _____
5. _____
6. _____

Task 4.12 Do You need HELP?

If Yes, why?

_____
_____
_____
_____
_____
_____
_____

If No, why?

_____
_____
_____
_____
_____
_____

Chapter 5
Rethinking Your Thinking

A major part of human nature or people involves thinking. More specifically, *how* you think (what we call the cognitive factors). Your deepest beliefs and thoughts provide the background template on the decisions you make. This is discussed below.

Cognitive Factors

There are a variety of factors that impact an individual's life, interactions, and experiences (e.g., emotional factors, behavioral factors, cognitive factors). Typically, cognitive frames involve specific core schemas described below and the typical cognitive distortions and tactics, also described below.

Basic cognitive distortions/thoughts, defenses or cognitive tactics include:

- Denial- not admitting too (defense and cognitive tactic)
- Lying-distorting information justifying – making it okay (cognitive tactic)
- Minimize- making less significant
- Entitlement-expecting to get desires met
- Power games – the illusion of the need of trying to control others (tactic)
- Extremes – either/or thinking
- Apathy – "don't care" attitude
- Blaming – external locus of control placing responsibility on others (tactic)
- Victim-stancing – self-pity/fallacy of fairness

There are specific implicit theories (core thinking) identified to be correlated with offending and otherwise (Bartels & Merdian, 2015; Polascheck & Ward, 2002; Ward & Keenan, 1999) including:

- Women are deceptive
- Disrespect towards some women
- Women/kids are primarily sex objects
- Illusion of control (one has to control others & context)
- Sees self as a victim
- Grievance & hostility towards others
- Views self as inadequate (poor self-esteem)
- Sex drive is uncontrollable
- Sexual entitlement

- Nature of harm (means NO harm, unless physical violence is used, thus minimizes impact)
- Dangerous world view (lack of trust, paranoia, adults=dangerous, need to control others)

The implicit theories commonly held by individuals who engage in rape (Polascheck & Ward, 2002) include:

- Women are unknowable or deceptive
- Women are sex objects
- Sex drive is uncontrollable
- Entitlement
- Dangerous world
- Power/control
- Inadequacy views
- Disrespectful to some females

The implicit theories commonly held by individuals who engage in sexual offenses towards children (Ward & Keenan, 1999) include:

- Children seen as sexual beings
- Nature farm
- Uncontrollable sex drive
- Entitlement
- Dangerous world

You have to figure out several things, such as, what type of thinking works when everything is cool or ok (life is working) versus when it is not versus when you are in an offending state. The next several tasks will help you sort it out. Thinking is indicated with your self-statements or self-talk. The keys to changing your thinking is changing your self-talk. You will learn how to defuse and change the thinking that doesn't work for you.

Task 5.1 What is your thinking like when all is going well?

1. _____

2. _____

3. _____

4. _____

5. _____
6. _____
7. _____
8. _____

Task 5.2 What is your thinking when all is not going well?

1. _____
2. _____
3. _____
4. _____
5. _____
6. _____
7. _____
8. _____

Task 5.3 What type of thinking is functional for you?

1. _____
2. _____
3. _____
4. _____
5. _____
6. _____
7. _____
8. _____

Task 5.4 Using information about the cognitive factors above, what type of thinking is dysfunctional for you?

1. _____
2. _____
3. _____
4. _____
5. _____
6. _____
7. _____
8. _____

Task 5.5 What type of thinking would someone engage in who engages in the sexual offending that initiated your treatment? (see list of cognitive factors)

1. _____
2. _____
3. _____
4. _____
5. _____
6. _____
7. _____
8. _____

Changing Your Dysfunctional (Stinking) Thinking

The best way to change your thinking is by identifying what you are telling yourself about whatever is going on and replacing bad thinking with rational thinking. Two key strategies are provided below.

Rational Emotive Behavioral Therapy (REBT)

REBT is a way to identify & challenge your thinking. You identify your irrational distorted thinking and challenge them by confronting them, thus, changing any irrational beliefs to more rational beliefs (Criddle, 1974; Dryden & Ellis, 1988; Ellis 1989; Ellis & Grieger, 1977). The method is simple and discussed below.

Basic REBT format: A B C D E

- A- Activating Event- the activating event is the triggering stimulus or situation
- B- Beliefs- are the connected thoughts linking perceptions about the specific events and/or life in general. There are either rational or irrational beliefs. Beliefs are often able to be tracked back to developmental events.
- C- Consequences- emotional or behavioral response or reaction (result).
- D- Disputing- basic key is identifying, challenging (speaking to see it), and confronting irrational beliefs changing the thought pattern. Disputing refers to confronting and challenging old beliefs. Replace the irrational belief with functional thoughts.
- E- Effective New Belief- after changing irrational thinking or distorted thinking to rational, monitor the outcome of the consequences.

This concept of REBT is the basis of rational emotive behavioral therapy. Therapy is used to change irrational thinking to rational clear thoughts. The process is: (a) event, (b) belief, (c) feelings, (d) dispute (or challenge) those thoughts, (e) behavior, (f) goals, and (g) action plan.

The process includes examining the event or situation and how one once thought about the situation; checking one's feelings about the situation; checking out any kind of distortions in one's thinking; and changing those distortions to rational thinking. At this time, clients can formulate a goal that one wants to achieve and make a detailed action plan of how to achieve this goal.

There are numerous types of thinking errors, distortions, and irrational beliefs. The key is to identify your distorted thinking, along with the effects and how to change it. There are several basic ways to do this. Most of society is based on distorted thinking. However, some distorted thinking hasn't help you. Therefore, as a coping strategy you can change it.

The essence of any cognitive restructuring approach involves identifying distorted thinking in self-talk and change it my replacing the thought.

Basic Cognitive Restructuring Approach

1. Identify the problem.

- The problem areas could range from arousal control, denial, responsibility, rage, self-destructive behavior, assault cycle behavior, etc.
- Once the problem behaviors are identified... go to the next steps.

2. Identify the triggering event.

3. Identify beliefs about the event and/or problem behaviors. Identify cognitive distortions.

    - Clues to dysfunctional thinking include the use of: awful, musts, shoulds, absolutes
    - Look for any extreme, absolute statements, and unrealistic expectations/demands.
    - Beliefs may be identified by tracking self-talk, such as by a tracking journal

4. Challenge dysfunctional thinking with functional thinking.

5. Replace distorted thinking with functional thinking.

6. Monitor outcome.

A variety of formats have been provided to help you restructure or change your dysfunctional beliefs and your irrational thoughts. Use the above counters to challenge your distorted thinking.

Task 5.6 List how you will restructure your thinking

_____
_____
_____
_____
_____
_____
_____
_____
_____
_____
_____
_____
_____

Task 5.7 List how you will stay with present and future responsibility

_____
_____
_____
_____
_____

_____
_____
_____
_____
_____
_____

Task 5.8: Use the REBT Format

Activating Events: _____

_____

_____

_____

Beliefs and Thoughts (including automatic thoughts): _____

_____

_____

_____

Consequences: _____

    Behaviors (if any): _____

_____

_____

    Feelings: _____

_____

_____

Dispute: _____

_____

_____

New Actions: _____

_____

_____

Task 5.9 Use the Basic Cognitive Restructuring Format

Instructions: (a) list a distortion, (b) put the definition next to it, and (c) list up to three counters for each

1. A. Distortion - _____

_____

   B. Counters

      1. _____

      2. _____

      3. _____

2. A. Distortion - _____

_____

   B. Counters

      1. _____

      2. _____

      3. _____

3. A. Distortion - _____

_____

   B. Counters

      1. _____

      2. _____

3. _____

4. A. Distortion - _____

_____

   B. Counters

      1. _____

      2. _____

      3. _____

5. A. Distortion - _____

_____

   B. Counters

      1. _____

      2. _____

      3. _____

Task 5.10 Use the Cognitive Reprogramming Format

Define Urge and/or Problem:

_____

_____

Identify your self-talk or what you are telling yourself about the urge. Then outline the consequence in terms of offending, deviance, etc. Next, mark if it is functional or dysfunctional in terms of the consequence.

(1) Self-Talk

_____

Consequence

_____

_____ Functional _____ Dysfunctional

(2) Self-Talk
_____

Consequence
_____

_____ Functional _____ Dysfunctional

(3) Self-Talk
_____

Consequence
_____

_____ Functional _____ Dysfunctional

(4) Self-Talk
_____

Consequence
_____

_____ Functional _____ Dysfunctional

(5) Self-Talk
_____

Consequence
_____

_____ Functional _____ Dysfunctional

You've identified the dysfunctional self-statements; now replace them with more functional ones. Remember your goals are to have no more victims, change deviant lifestyle, etc.

Task 5.11 Identify replacement statements to distorted thoughts.

My replacement statements are:

1. _____

2. _____

3. _____

4. _____

5. _____

6. _____

7. _____

8. _____

A list of example counter beliefs include:

- I make choices to offend or to hurt others when I do not have to
- I do not have to offend
- I can control myself
- I do not need excuses
- I do not have to feel sorry for myself
- I do not have the right to hurt others
- I can be rejected and still be okay
- I can be vulnerable and I'm okay
- Men do express feelings and remain okay

Task 5.12 Repetitive Listing Technique

Repetitive listing can help you change your thinking (scripts). Use your own paper simply list new beliefs in the form of short sentences and rewrite them 10 pages front/back. For example, write out "I choose to avoid self- pity" or "Life ain't fair & I'm ok". Use the "I choose…" format.

The essence of any cognitive restructuring approach involves identifying distorted thinking in self-talk and change it my replacing the thought.

Task 5.13 If you did do the offense, what would you be thinking?

1. _____

2. _____

3. _____
4. _____
5. _____
6. _____
7. _____
8. _____

Task 5.14 What would you replace that thinking with?

1. _____
2. _____
3. _____
4. _____
5. _____
6. _____
7. _____
8. _____

Chapter 6
Interpersonal Relationship Skills & Empathy

Basic Social Skills

Basic Conversational Skills

- This includes opening up a conversation, continuing or maintaining a conversation, and ending a conversation.
- Examples:
    - Opening up a conversation: "hello, how is it going,….".
    - Maintaining a conversation: finding common topics of interest or listening to the other persons interests.
    - Ending a conversation: saying "goodbye, perhaps good to see you. See you later…..".

Task 6.1 How would you open up a conversation? (practice with therapist)

_____
_____
_____
_____
_____
_____

Task 6.2 How would you continue a conversation? (practice with therapist)

_____
_____
_____
_____
_____
_____

Task 6.3 How would you end a conversation? (practice with therapist)

_____
_____
_____
_____

Listening Skills

- The listener or receiver allows the speaker or other person to feel understood.
- You may not want to use exact same words
- This requires indicating that other person is understood.
- Several common phrases include:
    - "I hear you saying…"
    - "It sounds like…"
    - "I understand you to say…"
    - "what you are saying…?"
    - "What I think you mean is…"

Task 6.4 Practice listening to others and write out how it feels and your thoughts.

Empathy

- Empathy is basically understanding what another is experiencing.
- Can be called perspective taking.
- Putting yourself in someone else's shoes and simply responding appropriately.

Task 6.5 Describe an experience when you have had empathy for someone.

_____
_____

With these skills you build relationships. Validating the other person, by acknowledging them helps.

Interpersonal Relationships

We are always involved in relationships. Whether we are in a dysfunctional or a functional state, you relate differently and are involved differently in relationships. Perhaps you isolate more. Perhaps you smother others. It is important to figure out how you respond in relationships when in your functional state versus dysfunctional state.

Task 6.6 What are your relationships like when you're dysfunctional state?

_____
_____
_____
_____
_____
_____
_____
_____

Task 6.7 Who are the individuals involved in your healthy relationships (functional) and why are they healthy?

_____
_____
_____
_____
_____
_____
_____
_____
_____

Interpersonal Issues

People in life have interpersonal issues. The less issues and the lesser degree of the problems, the more functional you are. Some of the following issues may play a role in your life:

- Possessiveness (owning what is not yours)
- Jealousy (wanting what someone else has)
- Control (the need to direct others)
- Enmeshment (boundaries that are entangled)
- Dependency (over-relying on others)

Task 6.8 What are your interpersonal issues? Circle the degree of the problem.

Note: The higher the number, the more problems.

- Possessiveness (owning what is not yours)   1 2 3 4 5 6 7 8 9 10
- Jealousy (wanting what someone else has)   1 2 3 4 5 6 7 8 9 10
- Control (the need to direct others)   1 2 3 4 5 6 7 8 9 10
- Enmeshment (boundaries that are entangled) 1 2 3 4 5 6 7 8 9 10
- Dependency (over-relying on others)   1 2 3 4 5 6 7 8 9 10

Task 6.9. List out any interpersonal issues that emerge in your relationships and describe them.

_____
_____
_____
_____
_____
_____
_____
_____
_____
_____
_____
_____
_____

Conflicts are natural in relationships because people are so different. Conflict resolution strategies are discussed below.

Conflict Resolution Strategies

Steps:
1. Know what you want
2. Respect the other person
3. Empathize & understand the other's position
4. Take ownership of your behavior
5. Relay your position (requests, expectations,...)
6. Identify others requests
7. Compromise—meet each other half-way.
8. Solidify agreement – even to agree to disagree

Task 6.10 Describe 3 times you have successfully used conflict resolution

1._____

2._____

3._____

Chapter 7
Regulation Skills & Mood Management

Emotions or feelings and anger/rage are a key part of your life plan. Regulating your moods are important in maintaining yourself.

Emotional Aspects

Typically, feeling states occur as primary emotions followed by secondary emotions that occur from basic feelings. The primary feelings include hurt/pain, sad, glad, scared, and bad while secondary feelings include anger, bad, apathy, confusion and anxiety. You need to distinguish these feelings states. They play a role when things are working/going right compared to when they are not.

Affective/Mood

Feelings connect together to form mood states. It is important for you to understand how you are feeling. Typically, there are primary feelings and then secondary feelings stemming from basic feelings (Carich, Huebner, Benhoff, 2020). A feeling is a physiological response or sensation with energy of some sort. It may seem automatic at times; however, it stems from thoughts. Some basic feeling states or categories include:

- Mad – anger to rage types of feelings
- Sad – depressed or feeling down
- Glad – happy, excited
- Bad – not feeling good or okay. This may include guilt, hurt, low self-worth, etc.
- Apathy – don't care attitude
- Confused – mixed up feelings
- Anxiety – nervous tension
- Hurt – victimize, being put down, hurt by others
- Scared – fears and insecurity

Most clients treat anger, depression inward. Remember at some level you are responsible for your behavior and mood. Feelings are not considered right or wrong; instead, it is what you do with them. One of the best ways to become more in tune with your feelings is to journal reactions about daily events.

Your thinking plays a role in your emotions. Distorted thinking is usually involved to some degree in your mood states. Thinking is indicated by self talk or self statements. Thinking can be automatic or spontaneous thinking. Blowing up involves thinking. Cognitive Distortions that can play a role in your mood include:

- Denial – non-admission
- Stuffing – ignoring, suppression, blocking out feelings
- Minimization – making less
- Justifying – excuses
- Blame – external locus of control
- Entitlement – unrealistic expectations
- Extreme Thinking – either/or, rigid
- Illusion of control – illusion one had to control to be okay
- Victim Stance – based on fairness fallacy; playing victim role in situations where not indicated

Task 7.1 What are you thinking when you have a good day?

_____
_____
_____
_____
_____
_____
_____
_____
_____
_____
_____

Task 7.2 What are you thinking when you have a bad day?

_____
_____
_____
_____
_____
_____
_____
_____
_____
_____
_____

Task 7.3 What can you do to change a bad day to an ok or even a good day?

_____

Task 7.4 What type of self talk? What do you tell yourself to change your mood?

_____

Task 7.5 What else can you do to regulate your emotions (coping skills)?

_____

Task 7.6 When are you in a dysfunctional state? What type of emotions do you feel?

Typically, several emotions stand out: mad – rage, apathy, feeling bad or had and perhaps confusion.

Task 7.7 What does your anger/rage state look like?

Task 7.8 What is the difference between your anger and risk for you?

Task 7.9. What type of primary feelings occur during a risk state?

Task 7.10 What type of thinking is involved in a risk state?

Identifying and Dealing with Anger

Anger is a feeling or emotion. As with any feeling, it is energy in the form of a physical reaction or sensation. Emotions move throughout one's body. A continuum is the best way to view anger (Cullen & Freeman-Longo, 1995). Anger can be evaluated or detected in degrees or levels ranging from frustration to rage.

.........I............................I...........................I...........................I..........................I............................I...

Frustration   Mild Anger   Anger   Extreme Anger   Hate   Rage

Anger serves a purpose. It is important for you to identify your anger and determine the purpose it serves for you.

As mentioned above, feelings can be viewed as primary and secondary. Primary feelings are those basic initial feelings experienced following thoughts. Secondary feelings are those feelings that follow others. Primary feelings include pain, rejection, abandonment, hurt of some type, loneliness, fear, and inferiority.

Secondary feelings include anger, rage, confusion, and resentment. The overall purpose of anger is the context, a compensation to a superior state. This means that you don't want to feel those basic feelings and think that you can gain control through anger.

It is important to distinguish between anger and aggression. Aggression is the behavior of reacting to your anger with victimizing intensity and violating someone else or destroying something. It is a provoked or unprovoked attack on another. It is doing something with anger. There are levels of anger intensity, ranging from mild anger to hostility. Anger may be instrumental or hostile. Instrumental anger is attacking someone to get something (Cullen & Freeman-Longo, 1995). For example, Jack Doe hits John Doe in order to get his stuff.

Task 7.11 Give four examples of instrumental anger from your life.

1. _____

2. _____

3. _____

4. _____

Task 7.12 Give four examples of hostile anger from your life.

1. _____
2. _____
3. _____
4. _____

Resentments build or are created because of unresolved anger.

Task 7.13 List your resentments and why you think these exist?

_____
_____
_____
_____
_____
_____
_____
_____
_____

Anger serves a purpose. Ultimately, anger is caused by the way you think about a situation. It could be because somebody said or did something that you were offended about and became angry. At some level it involves the reality of the situation and context, while at another level it involves your views of the event.

Task 7.14 What does anger do for you? List the purposes of you anger.

1. _____
2. _____
3. _____
4. _____
5. _____
6. _____
7. _____
8. _____

Good Points of Anger (Cullen & Freeman-Longo, 1995)

- A source of energy
- Helps you talk to others to relieve tension
- Gives you information
- Motivates you to control your life
- Motivates you to take action to resolve the problem

Task 7.15 Pick out the times when anger was healthy. See if you have used anger in a healthy way in the past or present.

1. _____
2. _____
3. _____
4. _____
5. _____
6. _____
7. _____
8. _____

Bad Functions of Anger:

- Stops you from functioning clearly
- Anger builds on anger – feeds itself, unless you defuse it
- Anger leads to negative expression
- Anger leads to rage and destructive behavior
- Anger leads into the sexual assault cycle

It is important to recognize when you are getting angry so that you can intervene. Chapter 5 deals with interventions. Some people are not aware of their anger, while other people are angry all the time. Cues help you identify anger states.

A cue is any type of signal, red flag, or warning that you are building (heating) up your anger. Cues can also be indicators that you are in an explosive situation and need to do something. Cues are warnings to you that you may be getting angry. If anger is your Targeted

Dysfunctional Behavior (TBD), then it is important to identify your earliest cues and stop the pattern or cycle at this point; it could be a sub-cycle as well. Chapter 5 provides a lot of details on cues. Cues can be directly applied to anger.

Task 7.16 What cues can you identify that indicate you would be or are angry? How can you tell when you are going to blow up? One way to track you anger patterns is to maintain anger logs.

1. _____
2. _____
3. _____
4. _____
5. _____
6. _____
7. _____
8. _____

The Basics of Intervention

An anger log is a specific type of journal that targets anger. Cullen and Freeman-Longo (1995) refer to it as a situation perception training (SPT). SPT is a learning process in which you think before you act. Part of the process is to track you anger. Cullen and Freeman-Longo's format is based on basic RET processes outlined below. These processes have been modified below.

Activating Event ----- Perception, interpretation based on belief system ------ Outcome Response

According to Ellis (1979) and others, it is not the event that upsets you, it is your belief about the event (Criddle, 1974). For instance, if someone calls you a derogatory name; then you now have a choice as to how you will respond. This is addressed in other chapters.

Interventions center around identifying anger and defusing it. The above intervention relies on changing beliefs/distortions/self-statements and replacing them with rational thoughts.

Chapter 8
Behavioral Impact & Empathy

People impact people differently. There are different impacts on people. It is the same with sexual behavior. Sexual behavior effects people differently. It is important, though uncomfortable, to look at sexual impacts. It could be very traumatizing for many, while not as bad for others. Few might not be affected.

Sexual Behavioral Impact

There can be all sorts of impacts on people. Sexual offending impacts each person differently. Each person is going to have a different perception of what happened. Perception and memories are subject to change. The reality of what happened can be confusing. That is why, sometimes, various versions of what happened may not all be the same.

List of Impact Behaviors (Carich, 1998)

Sexualized (become pre-occupied	Sexual Confusion	Physical Damage to the Victim
Identity Confusion	Prostitution	Alcoholism
Blames Self	Drug Abuse/Addictions	Guilt
Sexual Abuse	Multiple Personality	Psychosomatic Illness
Shuts Down and Can't Function	Sleep Disorders/Nightmares	Suicide
Shame	Suicidal Behavior	Phobias of All Sorts
Chronic Depression and Anxiety	Turned "on to"/Into a Perpetrator	Dissociative Behaviors
Chronic Anger	Self-Destructive Behaviors	Become Abusive/Angry/Hostile

These quotes all reflect victim responses. They are quoted from Freeman-Longo, Bays and Bear (1996):

- "The effects of sexual abuse go deep and last a lifetime."
- "The effects on each particular victim of sex abuse vary, but no victim goes unharmed. The damage is deep and much of it never goes away."

- "Victims of sexual abuse may be emotionally or mentally disabled with depression, rage, anxiety, uncontrollable behavior, feelings of powerlessness, sleep disorders, nightmares, flashbacks, sexual problems, prostitution, eating disorders, alcoholism, drug abuse, lack of self-esteem, lack of confidence, inability to motivate themselves, inability to say no, confusion, guilt, shame, self-hatred, self-mutilation, physical illness, excessive worry about health, withdrawal from loved ones, isolation and suicide."
- In essence, "the abuse can affect victims' lifestyles in many ways. Some victims are terrified to live in their own homes or neighborhoods and move when they can. Others are so uncomfortable around the type of individual who abused them... They avoid going certain places or meeting people who remind them in any way of the person who abused or raped them. Victims may fear the dark or being alone. Some can't brush their teeth or stand to go to the dentist because they were forced into fellatio. They may lose their families, friends, jobs and joyful activities..."
- "Sexual abuse also physically harms victims' bodies... can tear the victim's skin... can damage skin and muscle, dislocate joints, breast bones, suffocate and kill. Usually, victims fear for their lives. They may be so terrified that they vomit, urinate or defecate..."

Summary of Abusive Effects

This list is quoted from Freeman-Longo, Bays, and Bear (1996):

- "Distrust of others and themselves... fear of even gentle sex."
- "Terror and anxiety, hyper-vigilant (always nervously watchful)... fears of many kinds: of the dark, being alone with others, or sleep, nightmares, and flashbacks"
- "Shame, guilt and self-hatred... think... there is something wrong with them... boys wonder if they are gay, because they were abused"
- "Alienation from their bodies... Children's bodies respond to both non-sexual and sexual touch... may feel like their bodies betrayed them... Many abuse victims cope... by dissociating, spacing out or completely disconnecting from their bodies to the point that their only physical sensation is numbness...some victims cut, burn, otherwise mutilate their bodies in order to feel anything at all, or to try to let out the pain inside."
- "Isolation and withdrawal from people and activities... lonely... distrust... without self-esteem and confidence..."
- Powerlessness, depression and extreme passivity
- Anger... victims feel enraged
- "Obsession with sex or complete aversion to it. Some children who are sexually abused become sexualized...can lead to prostitution"

- Questioning their sexuality and gender
- Drug and alcohol use, abuse and addiction
- Eating disorders
- "Perfectionism and workaholism... as a way to keep their pain at bay"
- Mental illness and suicide
- Sexual offending

Long-Term Consequences

(Freeman-Longo et al., 1996)

- Fears
- Sexual dysfunction
- Relationship damage
- Depression
- Grief

In essence, people have different reactions and problems from offending. Typically, victims feel toxic shame, confusion and anger/rage stemming from hurt, anxiety, relationship issues, nightmares and other trauma-related behaviors, sexual identity issues, powerlessness, fears, embarrassment, drugs/alcohol, etc. Many may go into denial and try to minimize what happened, while others are crushed and devastated, and may never be the same.

Task 8.1 What do you think are some short-term effects?

1. _____
2. _____
3. _____
4. _____
5. _____
6. _____
7. _____
8. _____

Task 8.2 What do you think the long-term consequences are?

1. _____
2. _____
3. _____
4. _____
5. _____
6. _____
7. _____
8. _____

Task 8.3 If we acted "as if" you had engaged in sexual offending, what do you think these victims went through?

1. _____
2. _____
3. _____
4. _____
5. _____
6. _____
7. _____
8. _____

This section might be a bit painful and the most difficult to do. In this section, you will examine your behavior and the impact or consequences. Often it hurts to face the impact or consequences of our behavior onto others. It is important to have empathy for others, in general, and specifically for those you have hurt or offended. When hurting others, it is natural to feel bad. This is called remorse. Remorse is feeling guilt. Problems occur when people take it too far and extend it to themselves and their self-worth. This is called toxic shame. When you have poor self-esteem and poor self-worth these are risk factors. There are several models of empathy. There appears to be a number of elements in empathy for victims involving behavioral impact:

- Responsibility and reasonable thinking
- Harm recognition
- Emotional recognition
- Perspective taking
- Emotional expression
- Expressing normal remorse

The focus of change is enhancing your life plan so that this stuff doesn't happen again. In terms of empathy, change occurs along the above elements (Carich, May, & Huebner, 2020b). If you didn't actually do anything or you're claiming you didn't do anything, do the exercises as if you did and get a feel for what someone goes through when sexually violated.

In any of the assignments, nothing gets mailed, unless your therapist is in contact with the person impacted by your behavior and you agree to share the assignments. Complete the following tasks and processes with your therapist. It is important to process the tasks. In order to do these tasks, if you have violated a few different people then do this with each one. If you violated many, then perhaps pick the most severe or significant and do the exercises.

Task 8.4 Describe a sexual offending incident (either an offense you committed or an "as if" offense) and write out what happened from the perpetrator's view point and the view point of the person who was violated.

_____
_____
_____
_____
_____
_____
_____
_____
_____
_____
_____
_____
_____
_____

Task 8.5 Write a letter from a person whom was impacted by sexual violence as if they wrote it. Think about how they might be feeling about themselves and this situation. How has it impacted their life? How has it impacted their sense of safety? What is their idea of justice? What do they think needs to happen? How has it impacted their social relationships? If you didn't do it write a letter portraying their views

Task 8.6 Write an apology letter to that person "as if" you perpetrated the sexual violence (DO NOT GIVE IT or MAIL IT). An apology letter is not about asking for forgiveness from the person who was violated. Let the person who was violated know what steps you are taking to prevent yourself from engaging in sexual violence in the future. Acknowledge what you did and say "I'm Sorry." Let them know why you feel sorry.

_____
_____
_____
_____
_____
_____
_____
_____
_____
_____
_____
_____
_____
_____
_____
_____
_____
_____
_____

Task 8.7 With a therapist use apologetic imagery: Imagine yourself apologizing to the person who was hurt.

Task 8.8 How do you feel after completing Task 8.7?

_____
_____
_____
_____
_____
_____

_____
_____
_____
_____

In society, people are too much self-centered and don't seem to care about others. When you or anyone else is self-centered, often the impact of behaviors onto others gets largely lost. This set of exercises allows you to explore the impact that you have had and can have on others.

Chapter 9
Arousal Control & Sexual Regulation Skills

Sexual Fantasies

What is a sexual fantasy?

- Imagining or pretending a scenario that is not real, with a sexual theme, yet sexually arousing or stimulating (erotic).
- The scenario might be based on real events or memories

What's considered appropriate?

- A fantasy in which no one is disrespected, hurt, forced, or humiliated. Yet is sexually stimulating.
- A relationship based context

Positive Attitudes

- Your values
- Expectations of self and partner

Basic Rules

- Both parties need to agree
    - No threats, begging, badgering, physical force or violence, forcing
- There needs to be mutual respect for each other
- Your fantasy partner has to be age appropriate and consensual (agrees)
- A fantasy based upon a relationship context

Behavioral sequences

- The nature of the relationship
- What happens first (hopefully talking to each other)?
    - Behaviors: holding hands, caressing each other, holding each other, moves into foreplay
- What kind of foreplay?
    - Holding each other, touching/caressing, kissing
    - Fondling
- Sexual behaviors

– Fondling, oral sex, intercourse
- Afterwards
    – Touching, holding, talking

Physical/Emotional Parameters

- Looks/appearance of fantasy partner
- Facial Features (i.e. eyes)
- Built (height, weight, coloring...)

Exercises

- Outline your rules for a sexual encounter (healthy and appropriate)
- Outline the person in your fantasy (appearances)
- Outline the context of the fantasy (relationship)
- Outline the behavioral sequence (what happens)

Arousal Control & Sexual Regulation Skills

Some people will struggle with deviant urges or arousal. Arousal is an attraction to a person, animal or thing/object. Sexual arousal is sexual attraction. An urge is an immediate need to act out. A craving is a desire to fulfill something. You may need to use learning behavioral strategies to control your deviant arousal and defuse it. Several approaches are discussed.

Task 9.1 How do you currently regulate your sexual arousal?

1. _____
2. _____
3. _____
4. _____
5. _____
6. _____
7. _____
8. _____

Basic Conditioning

From behavioral "conditioning" or learning perspective there are several basic types of learning:

(1) Learning by association – called "classical conditioning," means learning by associating two items, images, experiences, behavior, stimulus, responses, etc. to get one event to elicit a selected response. One stimulus even can elicit a response.

(2) Items, images, experiences, behavior, stimulus, reinforcement, where responses are reinforced positively to occur again.

(3) Social learning – learning by observing and imitating others.

Covert Sensitization

Covert sensitization is a form of learning by association. Cautela (1985) uses the term covert sensitizations as a covert aversive conditioning process. Although sensitization refers to learning, covert sensitization refers to *unlearning* of one set of stimulus responses and *relearning* another set. You are sensitized to the aversive event in order to avoid the target response. Cautela stated:

> Covert sensitization is a cover conditioning procedure that is analogous to the operant conditioning procedure of punishment… The term covert is used because both the behavior to be reduced in frequency and the consequences are imagined by the individual. Sensitization designates that the individual is to be sensitized or taught to avoid a maladaptive approach response.

For example, you can learn to pair deviant urges with images of the pain inflicted on victims. This pairing interrupts the urge. Appropriate sexual urges and means of gratification can be covertly reinforced and covertly rehearsed. Ultimately you need to become desensitized from deviant urges/behaviors and re-sensitized to appropriate urges and behavior. You can continuously pair disgusting or painful images and stimuli to deviant urges or deviant responses. Learning occurs through association or pairings of things, events, and images. For example, offending responses/deviant behaviors (urges) can be paired with negative, unpleasant images. This pairing has to be done repeatedly. The pairing with anything negative ruins the urges. Ensure negative or punishing (gross/ugly/unpleasant) things are imagined.

Task 9.2 List one deviant response, negative image, and a result per item. The image may be anything (i.e., jail, empathy, pain, etc.)

1. Deviant response: _____

    Negative image: _____

    Result: _____

2. Deviant response: _____

    Negative image: _____

    Result: _____

3. Deviant response: _____

    Negative image: _____

    Result: _____

4. Deviant response: _____

    Negative image: _____

    Result: _____

5. Deviant response: _____

    Negative image: _____

    Result: _____

6. Deviant response: _____

    Negative image: _____

    Result: _____

7. Deviant response: _____

    Negative image: _____

    Result: _____

Cognitive Interventions

These tactics are based on what you are thinking. So, by changing your thinking (as in Chapter 5), you can defuse deviant thoughts and urges. Thinking can be very helpful. See chapter 5 for details.

Task 9.3 List out specific thoughts or self-statements that you can use to defuse deviant responses.

1. _____
2. _____
3. _____
4. _____
5. _____
6. _____
7. _____
8. _____
9. _____
10. _____

Task 9.4 List specific interventions that can be used to "counter" and "crash" lapses, urges, fantasies, responses, cravings, etc. Be specific.

1. _____
2. _____
3. _____
4. _____
5. _____
6. _____
7. _____

8. _____
9. _____
10. _____

Chapter 10
Addressing Trauma- Core Issues

Life is full of bumps, ups and downs, positive and negative/adverse experiences. Life experiences, both positive, neutral and negative occur throughout life. Those events that occur during critical developmental periods seem to make the most impact. Events viewed as positive appear to be more positive, while negative appear to be more negative. The biggest thing is how you viewed and view the event or experience. If you viewed it as positive, it probably was a good memory, while if viewed negative, then had an adverse experience and bad memory, resulting in an issue. Some developmental experiences occur more directly, meaning that you were directly involved versus indirectly. Indirectly means you observed it or were exposed to it and yet it still affected you. Sometimes negative experiences can be traumatizing resulting in issues or needs. Sometimes you might use anger, drugs, sex,… to fulfill these needs. Your thinking at the time of the experience and currently has everything to do with resolving the issue. The issues stem from life experiences and often get mixed up with sex (Carich & Kish, 2018). In this chapter, you will briefly outline any life experiences that maybe weren't the best and the resulting issues. This chapter needs to be done with a therapist, to help you work on these sensitive topics.

Task 10.1 Outline your difficult life experiences and the result (i.e. core issues):

1. Life Experience: _____

   _____

   Result/Impact: _____

   _____

2. Life Experience: _____

   _____

   Result/Impact: _____

   _____

3. Life Experience: _____

   _____

   Result/Impact: _____

   _____

4. Life Experience: _____
_____

    Result/Impact: _____
_____

5. Life Experience: _____
_____

    Result/Impact: _____
_____

6. Life Experience: _____
_____

    Result/Impact: _____
_____

7. Life Experience: _____
_____

    Result/Impact: _____
_____

8. Life Experience: _____
_____

    Result/Impact: _____
_____

Task 10.2 Review the results/impacts listed above. List the results/impacts above that you may identify as core issue(s) in your life (currently or in the past):

1. _____

2. _____

3. _____

4. _____

5. _____

6. _____

7. _____
8. _____

The key in resolving issues is letting go of the energy or negative emotions of the experience. This is done by pinpointing your thinking and changing it, thus releasing your energy. The key is that the event doesn't control you. You control you. It is based on how you think. Typically, people think that "life ain't fair & I'm not ok" or "my past controls me...". Change those beliefs instead to "life ain't fair (which is a fact) and I'm ok and I can deal with life" and "I control my behavior, not the past".

Task 10.3 List out your key beliefs

1. _____
2. _____
3. _____
4. _____
5. _____
6. _____
7. _____
8. _____

Task 10.4 Using the tactics in Chapter 5, list out your new beliefs

1. _____
2. _____
3. _____
4. _____
5. _____
6. _____
7. _____

8. _____

Another way to get rid of resentments is through forgiveness. Forgiving the person who wronged you can really help lift your burden.

Task 10.5 Write out the most significant event that happened to you. Do this process for each major event.

_____

Task 10.6 Write a forgiveness letter to the person or persons that hurt you deeply. Notice how the burden begins to lift (you are not sending/mailing the letter, this is an exercise).

_____

Using imagery

Task 10. 6 Practice imagery by following the steps below

- Pick out a metaphor that you associate with or represents strength, inner security, comfort, confidence
- Visualize or see in your mind
    - Imagine the strong image and feel the strength

- Feel the strength.
- Describe the experience to your therapist.
- Visualize the event and imagine the metaphor representing strength
  - Feel notice that you are okay and feel your own strength.
  - Describe the experience to your therapist.
- Visualize dealing with the situations and triggers (one at a time) that involve the trauma event.
  - Describe the experience to your therapist.
- See yourself mastering and feeling empowered concerning any negative life experience
  - Describe the experience to your therapist.
- See yourself in the future dealing with life events feeling okay.
  - Describe the experience to your therapist.

Task 10.7 Write about the imagery experience. What are some thoughts/feelings you had during the experience? Was this difficult/easy? How do you feel after completing the exercise?

_____
_____
_____
_____
_____
_____
_____
_____
_____
_____
_____
_____
_____
_____
_____
_____
_____

Task 10.8 Use imagery with your therapist to get rid of any other resentments following the steps below.

- Close your eyes and imagine a helium balloon with a big basket.
- Place your resentments or emotional garbage in the basket.
- Then cut the ties and watch your basket go up.
  - Feel the relief as the burdens are lifted.
- Watch the balloon get smaller and smaller until it disappears forever.

- See the basket tied down.
- Describe how you now feel.

Task 10.9 Write about the imagery experience.

_____
_____
_____
_____
_____
_____
_____
_____
_____
_____

Positive Pairing

Pleasant and positive things/images can be associated together and enable you to feel better about yourself. For example, imagining a picture of a lion, tiger, or eagle may give you a sense of inner strength. The same can be done for relaxation, self-image, inner peace, positive attitude, etc.

Task 10.10 List positive images or symbols for each of the items below and practice them and feel the inner source of pleasantness.

a. Images for self-confidence or appropriate inner strength

_____   _____
_____   _____
_____   _____

b. Images for relaxation

_____   _____
_____   _____
_____   _____

c. Images for self-image

_____   _____

_____   _____

_____   _____

d. Images for self-worth/esteem

_____   _____

_____   _____

_____   _____

e. Images for inner security

_____   _____

_____   _____

_____   _____

f. Images for countering stressors

_____   _____

_____   _____

_____   _____

Task 10.11 Outline some of your most positive experiences in your life and the resulting feelings.

_____
_____
_____
_____
_____
_____

_____
_____
_____

Task 10.12 What are your strengths?

1. _____
2. _____
3. _____
4. _____
5. _____
6. _____
7. _____
8. _____
9. _____

Task 10.13 What are you going to do to master the event or empower yourself?

1. _____
2. _____
3. _____
4. _____
5. _____
6. _____
7. _____
8. _____
9. _____

Chapter 11
Pattern Identification: Selecting Pathways

Behaviors can be dissected into patterns or pathways. Functional versus dysfunctional patterns/pathways within the offending subset are mapped out.

Identifying Your Functional vs. Dysfunctional Pathways

Pathways are nothing more that roads you are on. These roads include: your thoughts, feelings, behaviors, relationships, etc.. These are all intertwined into a pathway. When you are working good or are in decent shape emotionally or mentally, you think/feel/behave/relate differently than when you are not. The following tasks are based on what and how you think, feel, behave, and relate to others.

Task 11.1 When you are in a functional state, what does your life look like? How are you thinking? How are you feeling? What does your mind frame look like? (This is your functional pathway)

_____
_____
_____
_____
_____
_____
_____
_____
_____
_____
_____
_____
_____
_____

Task 11.2 When you are in a dysfunctional state, what does your life look like? How are you thinking? How are you feeling? What does your mind frame look like? (This is your dysfunctional pathway)

_____
_____
_____
_____
_____
_____
_____
_____
_____
_____

Task 11.3 When you are in a functional state, what do your interpersonal relationships look like?

- Who do you associate with?
- What are your interactions like?
- Level of conflicts?
- How is your intimate relationship going?

_____
_____
_____
_____
_____
_____
_____
_____
_____
_____

Task 11.4 When you are in a functional state, what kind of coping strategies/skills are you using? How do you deal with risk factors?

_____
_____
_____
_____
_____
_____
_____
_____
_____
_____
_____
_____

Task 11.5 When you are in a dysfunctional state, how do you meet your needs?

_____
_____
_____
_____
_____
_____
_____
_____
_____
_____
_____

Task 11.6 When you are in a dysfunctional state, what is your state of mind like? How are you thinking?

_____
_____
_____
_____

Task 11.7 When you are in a dysfunctional state, what are you feeling? What are you doing?

Identifying Offending Subset Pathways

It's important to tease out was going on with you and your offending pathways. For example, you have core issues, triggers, views thoughts feelings and behaviors. *Note:* This is based on "as if" you did, answer the questions below. These set of questions are to help you not get into this situation again/ever.

Task 11.8. List out your core issues:

_____
_____
_____
_____
_____
_____

Task 11.9 If you did it, what are your triggers/risk factors? Or, what would be your triggers/risk factors *if* you did it ("as if")?

1. _____
2. _____
3. _____
4. _____
5. _____
6. _____
7. _____
8. _____
9. _____
10. _____

Task 11.10 What are cues or warning signals that something is not right or reminders?

1. _____
2. _____
3. _____
4. _____
5. _____
6. _____

7. _____

8. _____

9. _____

10. _____

Task 11.11 What does your offending mind frame look like?

- A. Thoughts/Beliefs:
    1. _____
    2. _____
    3. _____
    4. _____
    5. _____
    6. _____
    7. _____
    8. _____
- B. Feelings:
    1. _____
    2. _____
    3. _____
    4. _____
    5. _____
    6. _____
    7. _____
    8. _____
- C. Behaviors:
    1. _____
    2. _____
    3. _____
    4. _____
    5. _____
    6. _____
    7. _____
    8. _____

D. Socially (who was around/involved in your life at that time):
   1. _____
   2. _____
   3. _____
   4. _____
   5. _____
   6. _____
   7. _____
   8. _____

E. Fantasies:
   1. _____
   2. _____
   3. _____
   4. _____
   5. _____
   6. _____
   7. _____
   8. _____

Task 11.12 If you did it, how would you set it up to happen (or answer as if you did it)?

1. _____

2. _____

3. _____

4. _____

5. _____

6. _____

7. _____

8. _____

Task 11.13 What do you get out of it?

1. _____
2. _____
3. _____
4. _____
5. _____
6. _____
7. _____
8. _____

Chapter 12
Meta-Change Maintenance: Preserving Change and Staying on Track

Effective coping responses are the keys to success. The authors view coping responses the same as interventions. Interventions are things you can do either in your mind or behaviorally in over to defuse any dysfunctional state/being. Some of this may seem repetitive; however, repetition really helps ingrain learning in your brain. You can't always do enough repetitions to ingrain learning. You really want some coping responses as automatic responses. In this chapter, we describe some of the more effective interventions.

Overview of Interventions

There are any number of interventions that can be used (Carich, 1991; Carich and Stone, 1996; Carich & Calder, 2003; Laws & Ward, 2006; Mann et al., 2004; Marshall et al., 2011; Pithers, 1990; Ward & Gannon, 2006; Ward et al.., 2004; Yates, 2008), categorized by experiential domains. They include: behavioral interventions, stimulus control (using avoidance, escape), cognitive restructuring, hypnotic, imagery, social, affective, role-play etc. Using interventions relies on self-awareness about functional and dysfunctional aspects of yourself and your patterns of offending.

For those who have lengthy offending histories, it is important that we develop specific ways to intervene this, especially focusing on three subsets: (a) arousal control, (b) mood management, and (c) impulse control. For those with few victims or primarily situational offenders, as well as anyone, it is important to maintain prosocial ways of functioning, which involve interventions and appropriate coping with life. This next section is divided into avoidant versus approach interventions.

Avoidant Strategies

This section was adapted from Carich and Cameron (2008). Avoidant strategies are inventions in which you control the trigger. Technically, this is referred to the "stimulus control." Stimulus control strategies involve actually controlling the environmental triggers. There are two basic types: avoidance and escape. People are so diverse and different that some will struggle with deviancy for life while others will not. Individuals that struggle with deviancy will have to avoid certain situations. The degree that you struggle with deviancy impacts the degree you need to avoid unnecessary risk situations for example if you have a chronic history of abusing children and struggle with those types of urges, you will have to avoid situations where you are unsupervised around children. These interventions are useful.

Avoidance/Escape Strategies

Many offenders with histories of offending and/or struggle with deviancy need to avoid situations involving possible or actual victim contact. For example, those that struggle with desires towards children need to stay away from children. They should avoid working at schools, going to playgrounds etc. Men struggling with raping women need to avoid risk factors that are associated with their patterns. For example, being out late at night, driving around aimlessly, hanging around in bars etc. The same is true for individuals who have chronic alcohol abuse/dependence. It is not a good idea to hang out in bars or even isolate in the mountains, even if you're not to planning to use. The same is for drugs; with drug addicts, it is advisable not to hang out with people actively using drugs. In doing so, research indicates that certain parts of the brain become stimulated or triggered to use. The same can be said for individuals that struggle with deviancy. Seemingly safe and otherwise simple decisions may easily escalate into high-risk situations.

Think about the situations and risk factors that you simply need to avoid in order to have a positive offense-free life. Is important to identify situations and factors to avoid. Also, think about situations that you may need to quickly get out or escape.

Task 12.1. List specific risk situations and or factors that you need to avoid.

_____
_____
_____
_____
_____
_____
_____
_____
_____
_____
_____
_____
_____

Task 12.2. List specific risks situation/factors that you need to escape from.

_____
_____
_____
_____

Approach Strategies

Basic Cognitive Restructuring Strategies and Tactics

As noted in Chapter 5, cognitive restructuring involves identifying problematic/distorted thoughts/distortions and then changing/countering the distortions by using rational thinking.

The basic cognitive restructuring format includes:

- Identify the problem.
    - The problem areas could range from arousal control, denial, responsibility, rage, self-destructive behavior, assault cycle behavior, etc.
    - Once the problem behaviors are identified… go to the next steps.
- Identify the triggering event.
- Identify beliefs about the event and/or problem behaviors (track self-talk, journal, etc.).
- Identify cognitive distortions.
- Challenge dysfunctional thinking with functional thinking.
- Replace distorted thinking with functional thinking.
- Monitor outcome.

A list of example counter beliefs is as follows:

- I make choices to offend or to hurt others when I do not have to
- I do not have to offend
- I can control myself
- I do not need excuses
- I do not have to feel sorry for myself
- I do not have the right to hurt others
- I can be rejected and still be o.k.

- I can be vulnerable and I'm o.k.
- Men do express feelings and remain o.k.

Clues to dysfunctional thinking include the use of: awful, musts, shoulds, absolutes

- Look for any extreme, absolute statements, and unrealistic expectations/demands.
- A variety of formats have been provided to help you restructure or change your dysfunctional beliefs and your irrational thoughts. Use the above counters to challenge your distorted thinking as you need.

Task 12.3 Basic cognitive restructuring activity. Instructions: (a) list a distortion, (b) put the definition next to it, and (c) list up to three counters for each. This is the same exercise completed for Task 5.9. Some of your distortions may still be the same, challenge yourself to think of others you may use.

1. A. Distortion - _____

_____

   B. Counters

      1. _____

      2. _____

      3. _____

2. A. Distortion - _____

_____

   B. Counters

      1. _____

      2. _____

      3. _____

3. A. Distortion - _____

_____

B. Counters

1. _____
2. _____
3. _____

4. A. Distortion - _____

_____

B. Counters

1. _____
2. _____
3. _____

5. A. Distortion - _____

_____

B. Counters

1. _____
2. _____
3. _____

Task 12.4 Identify replacement statements to distorted thoughts. Try to add some additional statements from those you offered in Chapter 5.

My replacement statements are:

1. _____
2. _____
3. _____
4. _____

5. _____

6. _____

7. _____

8. _____

The essence of any cognitive restructuring approach involves identifying distorted thinking in self-talk and changing it by replacing the thought.

Using Basic Conditioning

As first introduced in Chapter 7, from behavioral "conditioning" or learning perspective there are several basic types of learning:

(1) Learning by association – called "classical conditioning," means learning by associating two items, images, experiences, behavior, stimulus, responses, etc. to get one event to elicit a selected response. One stimulus even can elicit a response.

(2) Items, images, experiences, behavior, stimulus, reinforcement-- where responses are reinforced positively to occur again.

(3) Social learning – learning by observing and imitating others.

(4) Positive Pairing – pleasant and positive things/images can be associated together and enable you to feel better about yourself. For example, imagining a picture of a lion, tiger, or eagle may give you a sense of inner strength. The same can be done for relaxation, self-image, inner peace, positive attitude, etc.

Task 12.5: List positive images or symbols for each of the items below and practice them and feel the inner source of pleasantness. Recall images that you offered in Task 9.1, are these still relevant, or can you change/add.

a. Images for self-confidence or appropriate inner strength

_____   _____

_____   _____

_____   _____

b. Images for relaxation

c. Images for self-image

d. Images for self-worth/esteem

e. Images for inner security

f. Images for countering stressors

Covert Sensitization

As described in Chapter 7, covert sensitization is a form of learning by association. Cautela (1985) used the term covert sensitizations as a covert aversive conditioning process. Although sensitization refers to learning, covert sensitization refers to unlearning of one set of stimulus responses and relearning another set. You are sensitized to the aversive event in order to avoid the target response. For example, you can learn to pair deviant urges with images of the pain inflicted on victims. This pairing interrupts the urge.

Appropriate sexual urges and means of gratification can be covertly reinforced and covertly rehearsed. Ultimately you need to become desensitized from deviant urges/behaviors and re-sensitized to appropriate urges and behavior. You can continuously pair disgusting or painful images and stimuli to deviant urges or deviant responses. Learning occurs through association or pairings of things, events, and images. For example, offending responses/deviant behaviors (urges) can be paired with negative, unpleasant images. This pairing has to be done repeatedly. The pairing with anything negative ruins the urges. Ensure negative or punishing (gross/ugly/unpleasant) things are imagined.

Task 12.6 List one deviant response, negative image, and a result per number. The image may be anything (i.e., jail, empathy, pain, etc.). You may refer back to your responses from Task 9.2, challenge yourself to present below deviant responses, images, results that continue to present frequently or new deviant responses that have presented.

1. Deviant response: _____

    Negative image: _____

    Result: _____

2. Deviant response: _____

    Negative image: _____

    Result: _____

3. Deviant response: _____

    Negative image: _____

    Result: _____

4. Deviant response: _____

    Negative image: _____

    Result: _____

5. Deviant response: _____

   Negative image: _____

   Result: _____

6. Deviant response: _____

   Negative image: _____

   Result: _____

7. Deviant response: _____

   Negative image: _____

   Result: _____

8. Deviant response: _____

   Negative image: _____

   Result: _____

Task 12.7 List specific relapse interventions that can be used to "counter" and "crash" lapses, urges, fantasies, responses, cravings, etc. Be specific.

1. _____
2. _____
3. _____
4. _____
5. _____
6. _____
7. _____
8. _____

Cognitive Behavioral Interventions

Cognitive-behavioral refers to combining thinking and behavior as an intervention. Typical interventions include keeping journals, writing out goals/plans, keeping notes, etc.

A series of tasks have been provided as well. This will help you maintain a "good life" and pro-social attitude. It is important to establish effective goals with plans and stick to them. You can write scripts for your future, which is what the last several chapters consist of.

Task 12.8 Reminder Cards

Reminder Notes of Plans

Fill out index cards with your basic plans concerning what you are going to do when you encounter a triggering event. Carry them with you at all times. For example: (a) recognize triggers, (b) monitor self-talk and feelings, (c) avoid/escape the situation, and (d) interrupt relapse.

1. _____
2. _____
3. _____
4. _____
5. _____
6. _____

Reminder Notes of Goals

Notes of your goals can be placed all over your room or living area.

1. _____
2. _____
3. _____
4. _____
5. _____
6. _____

Reminder Notes of Dysfunctional and New Functional Self-Talk

Dysfunctional:

1. _____
2. _____
3. _____
4. _____
5. _____
6. _____

Functional:

1. _____
2. _____
3. _____
4. _____
5. _____
6. _____

Reminder Notes of Philosophical Statements

Notes containing special philosophical sayings, statements, slogans, etc.

1. _____
2. _____
3. _____
4. _____
5. _____
6. _____

Reminder Notes of Positive Messages

Notes with positive messages on them

1. _____
2. _____
3. _____
4. _____
5. _____
6. _____

Miscellaneous Reminder Notes

Any message can be put on reminder notes. Reminders notes reinforce the new (futuristic) programming or relapse information.

1. _____
2. _____
3. _____
4. _____
5. _____
6. _____

Imagery

Imagery refers to the internal visualization and representation of behaviors, thoughts, feelings, behavioral sequences, etc. with themes. Imagery may consist of a single image or themes and sequences of events. For example, offenders may be instructed to rehearse, through imagery, the futuristic projection of self-coping feelings of confidence and ego strength. This reinforces self-efficacy. Imagery techniques are most effective when using the sensory modes (sight, sound, feeling, movement, smell).

Imagery is an envisioning process that is a normal part of experience. If you have negative imagery, then you will have negative experiences. If you have positive imagery, then you will have positive experiences. Imagination and fantasy consist of the imagery processes.

It is important to generate a pool of interventions for your key triggers. It is even better to ingrain key intervening responses. What are your key intervening responses?

Task 12.9: List your key intervening responses.

1. _____
2. _____
3. _____
4. _____
5. _____
6. _____
7. _____
8. _____
9. _____
10. _____

Social Network

Socializing and relationships are part of society. You cannot avoid people. Relationships range on a variety of levels, from casual acquaintances to good, close friends. The people you associate with can be and are influential in your life. If you hang out with negative influences, then you may engage in negative criminal behavior. If you hang out with positive people or have positive relationships, then you likely have positive, productive, and functional relationships. If you isolate, then that is a problem. Risk factors connected to re-offending include (a) isolation and (b) negative peer network.

Task 12.10 Whom do you currently associate with? Rate the closeness of the relationship as well as how positive the relationship is.

Name	Nature of Relationship	Closeness (1-10)	Positive (1-10)

Task 12.11 Take the names in the table and describe the relationship.

1. _____

2. _____

3. _____

4. _____

5. _____

6. _____

7. _____

8. _____

9. _____

10. _____

Interpersonal Issues

People in life have interpersonal issues. The less issues and the lesser degree of the problems, the more functional you are. Some of the following issues may play a role in your life:

- Possessiveness (owning what is not yours)
- Jealousy (wanting what someone else has)
- Control (the need to direct others)
- Enmeshment (boundaries that are entangled)
- Dependency (over-relying on others)

Task 12.12 Describe how you will deal with each that are problems?

- Possessiveness (owning what is not yours)

    _____
    _____
    _____

- Jealousy (wanting what someone else has)

    _____
    _____
    _____

- Control (the need to direct others)

    _____
    _____
    _____

- Enmeshment (boundaries that are entangled)
  _____
  _____
  _____

- Dependency (over-relying on others)
  _____
  _____
  _____

Task 12.13 Plans for Meeting Your Needs and Managing Impulses. We all have needs. It is important to make plans of how you are going to meeting your needs.

Meeting Your Emotional Needs

Everyone has emotional needs. Prescott (2018) emphasizes ways of doing that include: respect, understanding feelings of others, being free of conflict, maintain emotions through activities. How are you going to regulate your emotions? More specifically how are you going to handle anger/hostility or even rage?

1. _____
2. _____
3. _____
4. _____
5. _____

Meeting Your Sexual Needs

Appropriate ways to meet needs of sexual satisfaction

1. _____
2. _____
3. _____
4. _____
5. _____

Meeting Your Health Needs

Plans to being physically healthy or taking care of self

1. _____
2. _____
3. _____
4. _____
5. _____

Impulse Control Plan

How you are going to deal with impulse control

1. _____
2. _____
3. _____
4. _____
5. _____

Sexual Arousal Control Plan

How are you going to control your sexual arousal?

1. _____
2. _____
3. _____
4. _____
5. _____

Deviant Arousal Control

If you did it (or "as if" you did it), how are you going to regulate or control your deviant arousal?

1. _____
2. _____
3. _____
4. _____
5. _____

Task 12.14 Complete your Life Risk Management Plan

Life Management Plan

A life risk management plan is your personal plan on how you are going to manage your life. That means how you are going to meet key needs and deal with key risk factors.

1. Needs/goals

    A. What type relationships do you want to have?

    _____
    _____
    _____
    _____

2. Work & skills- job skills & activities in which one gets paid

    A. What type of job skills do you have?

    _____
    _____
    _____
    _____

    B. What type of jobs do you want?

    _____
    _____
    _____
    _____

C. What type of jobs would you settle for?

3. Play/leisure- recreational activities
   A. What type recreational skills do you have?

   B. What type of recreational activities do you like?

4. Inner Peace- free from inner emotional turmoil & anxiety

   A. What does inner peace mean to you?

   B. How can have inner peace?

1. Health- taking care of self physically
   A. How do you take care of self?

2. Spirituality- connection to a higher power, larger than self &/or meaning of one's life?
   A. What does this mean to you?

   B. What is the meaning of your life at this point?

   C. How can you get there?

I. Key Interventions to maintain a functional state including thinking and behaviors

1. _____
2. _____
3. _____
4. _____
5. _____
6. _____
7. _____
8. _____
9. _____

10. _____

II. Key risk factors, cues, and interventions

    A. Impulsive decisions
       Cues_____

    Interventions:

       1._____
       2._____
       3._____
       4._____
       5._____

    B. Sexual deviant arousal
       Cues_____

    Interventions:

       1._____
       2._____
       3._____
       4._____
       5._____

    C. Mood management
       Cues_____

    Interventions:

       1._____
       2._____
       3._____
       4._____
       5._____

III. Situations to avoid and/or escape from:

1. _____

2. _____

3. _____

4. _____
5. _____
6. _____
7. _____
8. _____
9. _____
10. _____

Chapter 13
Concluding Thoughts

This manual offers plans for a reasonable set of ways to address difficult issues such as deviancy without directly addressing or admitting to deviancy. Change is creating a difference at some level and creating dimension through an experiential domain. Your life is your life. You can live it anyway you want. You have your whole life ahead of you. You need to decide how you are going to live it. What do you want to do? How do you see your future?

Task 13.1 List out how you see your future by your goals in life.

1. _____
2. _____
3. _____
4. _____
5. _____
6. _____
7. _____
8. _____
9. _____
10. _____

Task 13.2 Talk about what you've learned from completing this workbook. (About yourself, relationships, your feelings, your thoughts, etc……)

_____
_____
_____
_____
_____
_____
_____

References

Adler, A. (1941). *Understanding human nature.* World Publishing.

Adler, A. (1956). *The individual psychology of Alfred Adler.* In Ausbacher, H. & Ausbacher, R. (Eds.) *The Individual Psychology of Alfred Adler.* Basic Books.

Barbaree, H. E., Langton, C. M., Blanchard, R., & Boer, D. P. (2008). Predicting recidivism in sex offenders using the SVR-20: The contribution of age-at release. *International Journal of Forensic Mental Health, 7*(1), 47-64.

Bartels, R. M., & Merdian, H. L. (2015). The implicit theories of child sexual exploitation materials users: An initial conceptualization. *Aggression and Violent Behavior,* https://doi.org/10.1016/j.avb.2015.11.002

Bays, L., & Freeman-Longo, R. (2000). *Why did I do it again? And how can I stop?* NEARI Press.

Carich, M. S. (1991). Relapse interventions: A brief review. *INMAS Newsletter, 4*(3), 7-11.

Carich, M.S. (1998). The third alternative: A meta-recursive view. *The Milton Erickson Foundation Newsletter, 8,* 2.

Carich, M. S., & Calder, M. C., & Martin, C. (2003). *Contemporary treatment of adult male sex offenders.* Russell House Press.

Carich, M. S., & Cameron, B. (2008). Identifying the assault cycle and intervention skills. In B. Schwartz (Ed.) *The Sex Offender: Corrections, Treatment, and Legal Developments.* Civil Research Institute.

Carich, M. S., & Dobkowski, G. (2007). Clinical and theoretical notes on the change process for sexual offenders. *ATSA Forum, 19.*

Carich, M.S., Huebner, J., & May, K. (2020). *Training Manual: Offense Pathways & Mind Frames: Identifying Offending Pathways.* Carich, Huebner, & May.

Carich, M. S., Huebner, J., & Loy, T. (2020). Re-categorization of Mann's meaningful dynamic risk factors. *ATSA Forum, 39*(4).

Carich, M. S. & Kish, H. (2018). Utilizing Covert Conditioning Techniques to Increase and Decrease Targeted Behavior. *The ATSA Forum Newsletter. XXX, (1),* Winter.

Carich, M. S., May, K. & Huebner, J. (2020a). *Training Manual: The Basics of Understanding Men Who Offend: Definitions, Types & Theories. Volume II: Evaluation & Assessment.* Carich, May, & Huebner.

Carich, M. S., May, K. & Huebner, J. (2020b). *Training Manual: Enhancing Empathy For Others & Victims: Basic & Advanced Skills.* Carich, May, & Huebner.

Carich, M. S. & Stone, M. (1996). Sex Offender Relapse Intervention Workbook [Presentation]. Adler School of Professional Psychology, Chicago, IL, United States.

Cautela, J. R. (1985). Covert sensitization. In A. Bellack & M. Herson (Eds.) *Dictionary of Behavior Therapy Technique.* (p. 96). Pergamon Press.

Criddle, W. D. (1974). Guidelines for challenging irrational beliefs. *Rational Living, 9*(1), 8-13.

Cullen, M., & Freeman-Longo, R. (1995). *Men and anger: A relapse prevention guide to understanding and managing your anger.* Safer Society Press.

Dreikurs, R. (1967). *Psychodynamics, psychotherapy, and counseling.* Alfred Adler Institute.

Dryden, W., & Ellis, N. (1988). Rational-emotive therapy. In K. Dobson (Ed.), *Handbook of Cognitive Behavioral Therapies* (pp. 214-272). The Guilford Press.

Ellis, A. (1989). Rational emotional therapy. In A. Corsini, & D. Wedding. (Eds). *Current psychotherapies.* (pp. 197-238). Peacock.

Ellis, A., & Grieger, R. (1977). *Handbook of rational-emotive therapy.* Springer.

Freeman-Longo, R., Bays, L., & Bear, E. (1996). *Empathy and Compassionate Action Issues and Exercises: A Guided Workbook for Clients in Treatment.* The Safer Society Press.

Hanson, R. K., & Bussiere, M. T. (1998). Predicting relapse: A meta-analysis of sexual offender recidivism studies. *Journal of Consulting and Clinical Psychology, 66*, 348-362.

Hanson, R. K., & Harris, A. J. R. (2001). A structured approach to evaluating change among sexual offenders. *Sexual Abuse: A Journal of Research and Treatment, 13*, 105-122.

Hanson, R. K., & Morton-Bourgon, K. E. (2005). The characteristics of persistent sexual offenders: A meta-analysis of recidivism studies. *Journal of Consulting and Clinical Psychology, 73*, 1154 – 1163.

Laws, D. R., & Ward, T. (2006). When one size doesn't fit all: The reformulation of relapse prevention. In W. L. Marshall, Y. M. Fernandez, L. E. Marshall, & G. A. Serran (Eds.) *Sexual Offender Treatment: Controversial Issues.* (pp. 241-254). John Wiley & Sons.

Longo, R. F. (2002). A holistic/integrated approach to treating sexual offenders. In B. K. Schwartz (Ed.). *The Sexual Offender: Current Treatment Modalities and Systems Issues, Volume IV* (Chapter 21). Civic Research Institute.

Lund, C.A. (2000). Predictors of sexual recidivism: Did meta-analysis clarify the role and relevance or denial? *Sexual Abuse: A Journal of Research and Treatment, 12*(4), 275-287.

Mann, R. E., Hanson, R. & Thornton, D. (2010). Assessing risk for sexual recidivism: Some proposals on the nature of psychological meaningful risk factors. *Sexual Abuse: A Journal of Research and Treatment, 22*(2), 191-217.

Mann, R., Webster, S., Schofield, C., & Marshall, W. L. (2004). Approach vs. avoidance goals in relapse prevention with sexual offenders. *Sexual Abuse: A Journal of Research & Treatment, 16*(1), 65-75.

Marshall, W.L., Marshall, L.E. Serran, G.A., & Fernandez, Y.M. (2006) *Treating sexual offenders: an integrated approach.* Routledge.

Marshall, W.L., Marshall, L.E., Serran, G.A., & O'Brien, M.D. (2011). *Rehabilitating sexual offenders: A strengths based approach.* Washington, DC: American Psychological Association.

Marshall, W.L., Marshall, L. E., Serran, G.A., & Fernandez, Y.M. (Eds.). (2006). *Sexual offender treatment: Controversial issues.* John Wiley & Sons.

Marshall, W. L., Marshall, L. E., Serran, G. A., & O'Brien, M. D. (2011). *Rehabilitating sexual offenders: A strengths based approach.* American Psychological Association.

McGrath, R. J., Cumming, G. F. & Lasher, M. P. (2013). *SOTIPS Sexual Offender Treatment Intervention & Progress Scale Manual.*

McMurran, M. & Ward, T. (2004). Motivating offenders to change in therapy: An organizing framework. *Legal & Criminological Psychology, 9,* 295-311.

Nunes, K.L., Hanson, R.K., Firestone, P., Moulden, H.M., Greeberg, D.M., & Bradford, J.M. (2007). Denial predicts recidivism for some sexual offenders. *Sexual Abuse: A Journal of Research and Treatment, 19,* 91 – 105.

Pithers, W. D. (1990). Relapse prevention with sexual aggressors: A method for maintain therapeutic gain and enhancing external supervision. In W. L. Marshall. *Handbook of Sexual Assault: Issues, Theories, and Treatment of the Offender* (Ed.) (pp. 343-361). Plenum Press.

Polaschek, D. L., & Ward, T. (2002). The implicit theories of potential rapists: What our questionnaires tell us. *Aggression and Violent Behavior, 7,* 385-406.

Prescott, D. (2018). *Becoming who I want to be: A good lives workbook for young men.* Safer Society Press.

Prochaska, J. O., & DiClemente, C. C. (1982). Transtheoretical therapy: toward a more integrative model of change. *Psychotherapy, Theory, Research, and Practice, 19,* 276-288.

Schneider, S. L., & Wright, R. C. (2004). Understanding denial in sexual offenders: A review of cognitive and motivational processes to avoid responsibility. *Trauma Violence & Abuse, 5*(1), 3-20.

Ward, T. (2002). Good lives & the rehabilitation of offenders: Promises & problems. *Aggression & Violent Behavior, 7,* 513-528.

Ward, T., & Gannon, T. (2006). Rehabilitation, etiology, and self-regulation: The Good Lives Model of sexual offender treatment. *Aggression and Violent Behavior, 11,* 77-94.

Ward, T., & Hudson, S.M. (1998). A model of the relapse process in sexual offenders. *Journal of Interpersonal Violence, 13,* 700-725.

Ward, T., & Hudson, S. (2000). A self-regulation model of relapse prevention. In D. R. Laws, S. Hudson, & T. Ward (Eds.). *Remaking relapse prevention with sex offenders: A sourcebook.* (pp 79-101). Sage.

Ward, T., & Keenan, T. (1999). Child molesters' implicit theories. *Journal of Interpersonal Violence, 14*(8), 821-838.

Ward, T. & Marshall, W.L. (2004). Good lives, etiology, and the rehabilitation of sex offenders a bridging theory. *Journal of Sexual Aggression, 10,* 153-69.

Ward, T., & Stewart, C. (2003). Good lives and the rehabilitation of sexual offenders. (Eds). *Sexual Deviance: Issues and Controversies.* Sage.

Watzlawick, P., Weakland, J., & Fisch, R. (1974). *Change: The principles of problem formulation and problem resolution.* Garland.

Yates, P. (2008). Good lives, self-regulation, and risk management: An integrated model of sexual offender assessment and treatment. *Sexual Abuse in Australia and New Zealand: An Interdisciplinary Journal, 1,* 3-20.

Yates, P. M. (2009). Is sexual offender denial related to sex offence risk and recidivism? A review & treatment implications. *Psychology, Crime & Law, 15* (2, 3), 183-199.

Yates, P., Prescott, D., & Ward, T. (2010). *Applying the good lives and self-regulation models to sex offender treatment: A practical guide for clinicians.* Safer Society Press.

Made in the USA
Coppell, TX
13 October 2024